# GHOST OF KENT

FOR

FREDERICK W.T. SANDERS

Kentish Ghost Hunter Extraordinaire
and friend for twenty years

*By the same author*
This Haunted Isle (Harrap)
The Ghost Hunters (Robert Hale)
Dictionary of the Supernatural (Harrap and Fontana)
Haunted London (Harrap and Fontana)
Into the Occult (Harrap and Tandem)
Deeper Into the Occult (Harrap)
A Gazetteer of British Ghosts (Souvenir Press and Pan)
A Gazetteer of Scottish and Irish Ghosts (Souvenir Press and Fontana)
Ghosts of Wales (Christopher Davies and Corgi)
Hauntings: New Light on Ten Famous Cases (Dent)
A Host of Hauntings (Leslie Frewin)
The Vampire's Bedside Companion (Leslie Frewin and Coronet)
Ghosts of North West England (Collins/Fontana)
The Complete Book of Dowsing and Divining (Hutchinson)
A Ghost Hunter's Handbook (Hutchinson/Sparrow)
Ghosts of Devon (Bossiney Books)
Ghosts of Cornwall (Bossiney Books)
Ghosts of Hampshire and the Isle of Wight (St Michael's Abbey Press)

*Autobiography*
No Common Task — the Autobiography of a Ghost Hunter (Harrap)

*With Paul Tabori*
The Ghosts of Borley: A Critical History of 'the most haunted house in England' (David & Charles)

*With Leonard Wilder*
Lives to Remember: A Case Book on Reincarnation (Robert Hale)

*Biography*
Horror Man — the Life of Boris Karloff (Leslie Frewin)
Life's a Drag: A Life of Danny La Rue (Leslie Frewin)

*As Editor*
Thirteen Famous Ghost Stories (Dent's Everyman's Library)

# GHOSTS OF KENT

Authentic ghost stories from the Garden of England

by

PETER UNDERWOOD

President of The Ghost Club

Meresborough Books

Published by Meresborough Books, 17 Station Road, Rainham, Kent, ME8 7RS.

Meresborough Books is a specialist publisher of books about Kent with about a hundred titles currently in print. Full list sent on request.

In 1979 Meresborough Books launched a monthly magazine 'Bygone Kent'. Each issue contains about a dozen articles on a variety of different topics. It is available in local bookshops and newsagents or by postal subscription. The current rate (1992) is £21.00 for twelve issues (£26.00 overseas). A gift subscription makes a present that lasts a whole year.

© Copyright 1985 Peter Underwood

ISBN 0905270 86 X

Reprinted 1987 and 1992

Printed and bound in Great Britain by
Biddles Ltd, Guildford and King's Lynn

# FOREWORD

For millions of years Kent lay buried under the sea. The shrinking crust of the earth gave Kent its great whaleback of chalk, the glorious North Downs and the wonderful Weald of Kent — once a vast forest, the Andredsweald of the Anglo Saxons.

The climate of Kent is distinctive, warmer and kinder than most counties in Britain. Kent may well have escaped, by the width of the Thames estuary, the great ice-sheet that crept over Northern Europe after Pleiocene times and so Kentish people have perhaps lived in these islands longer than anyone with the result that their natures, their beliefs, superstitions and their knowledge are all of an older standing and may be linked, as no other inhabitants of Britain, to prehistoric ways and emotions and race-memories.

Kent was the first of the English kingdoms and it has preserved the earliest British names: the Cantii were the ancient Britons in possession here and Cantibury was their chief town when Julius Caesar landed. Rochester is another of the oldest towns in England.

The men of Kent and Kentish men, combined, are a race on their own; staunch men and true, the farmers producing crops and fruit of many kinds, their sheep and cattle grazing the sheltered pasturelands; the city man returning as soon and as often as he can to the fair lady of the English counties where a group of cowled oasthouses set among hop fields breathes the very life of Kent.

Relics from the Old Stone Age (6,000 years before Christ) the Roman occupation and every succeeding age have been found in Kent and men from Chaucer to Churchill have trod the age-old Pilgrims Way winding its way at the foot of the Downs.

Each of these climatic upheavals, historical associations and unique conditions; each of these ages and not a few of the singular personages who knew Kent at some period of its long history has, curiously and inexplicably but unmistakably, contributed to the wealth of psychical happenings reported from this lovely part of England.

Here may be found ghosts of Roman soldiers, Royal ghosts from many ages, ghosts of nuns and monks, of murderers and the murdered, of suicides, identified and unidentified men in comparatively modern suits and recognised and unrecognised ladies, some happy, some sad and some carrying flowers; there are ghostly animals and phantom coaches and horses . . . the list is endless.

Most of the grand houses of Kent have their ghosts, as have many of the old inns and hostelries — not a few dating from smuggling days. Country churches, rectories, ruins and mellow houses tucked into the folds of the quiet hills and valleys have their ghosts, sometimes but not always associated with some tragic or violent event of the past; at other times unremarkable and illogical as far as we know. As with every other part of the world the ghosts of Kent are bewildering in their variety and fascinating in their frequency.

During this tour of the ghostland of Kent I have tried to present a representative selection of the rich harvest of ghost material that is available. There are many more accounts of ghostly manifestations that I could have included and many, I am sure, that I have yet to hear about; but I shall long remember happy ghost hunting days in glorious Kent.

Peter Underwood

The Savage Club,
Berkeley Square,
London, W.1.


## Select Bibliography

Braddock, Joseph. *Haunted Houses* Batsford, 1956
Brown, Raymond Lamont. *Phantoms of the Theatre* Satellite Books, 1978
Church, Richard. *Kent* Robert Hale, 1948
Coxe, Antony D. Hippisley. *Haunted Britain* Hutchinson, 1973
Davison, Ian. *Where Smugglers Walked* Herbert Jenkins, 1935
Fea, Allan. *Rooms of Mystery and Romance* Hutchinson, 1931
Fedden, Robin. *Churchill and Chartwell* National Trust, 1968
Forman, Joan. *The Haunted South* Robert Hale, 1978
Green, Andrew. *Ghosts of Today* Kaye & Ward, 1980
Green, Andrew. *Ghosts of Tunbridge Wells* John Hilton, 1978
Green, Andrew. *Shire Album: Haunted Houses* Shire Publishers, 1975
Halifax, Lord. *Ghost Book* Geoffrey Bles, 1936
Hallam, Jack. *The Ghost Tour* Wolfe Publishing, 1967
Mackenzie, Andrew. *Hauntings and Apparitions* Heineman, 1982
Mackenzie, Andrew. *The Unexpected* Arthur Barker, 1966
Mee, Arthur. *Kent: The King's England* Hodder & Stoughton, 1969
Price, Harry. *Fifty Years of Psychical Research* Longmans, Green, 1939
Price, Harry. *Poltergeist Over England* Country Life, 1945
Sanders, Frederick. *Haunted Kent* (unpublished typescript), 1946
Shears, W.S. *This England* Hutchinson, 1948
Underwood, Peter. *A Gazetteer of British Ghosts* Souvenir Press, 1971
Underwood, Peter. *A Host of Hauntings* Leslie Frewin, 1973
    also various newspapers, magazines and periodicals including *Bygone Kent*

## ACKNOWLEDGMENTS

The author gratefully acknowledges the help he has received from many people and especially from:

G.B. Boreham, Reference Librarian at Folkestone for his researches in respect of Underhill House, Chatham; and all the other librarians, owners, custodians, administrators and historians who have helped him.

C.T. Fleetway of Canterbury for his first-hand account of seeing an unexplained figure.

Kevin Griffin for considerable help and co-operation in respect of his investigations in the Tunbridge Wells and Tonbridge areas — enquiries in which his brother Sean helped.

Nigel and Diana Gunnis for showing him their charming home.

Mrs Elizabeth Hussey of Scotney Castle for being so helpful.

Air Commodore R.C. Jonas OBE for so kindly allowing him access to his files.

Andrew Jupp for an account of his experiences at Pluckley.

Mrs Keen for allowing him to absorb the atmosphere of her home.

Steuart and Freda Kiernander for accompanying him on some of his visits to haunted houses in Kent.

Brigadier J.A. Mackenzie CBE, DSO, MC for his stories of ghosts at Slaybrook.

Eric Maple for a note of his experiences at Lympne Castle.

Mrs Joan Marks for an account of her experience at The Old Hall, Rochester.

Frederick Sanders for his friendship over many years and for allowing him to use and quote from his manuscript about his ghost hunts in Kent.

Miss Joyce Sewell of Honiton for the story of a persistent ghost.

Donald West for information about the ghost at the Royal Oak, Hawkhurst. His son Chris for the loan of some books from his library, and to his wife Joyce Elizabeth for accompanying him on his visits to Kent and for so much more besides.

Back Cover:
    The author   (Photo: Ian Hossack)

Hall Place, Bexley

## Aldington Corner

Sinister events at The Walnut Tree inn a century and a half ago have left behind the sounds of murder. In the days when smuggling of contraband was a profitable and popular occupation in these parts this inn was used as their headquarters by George Ransley and his two sons, who were almost as famous for their daring and impudence as the Hawkhurst gang who operated elsewhere in the county. From a window at the back of the inn accomplices on Romney Marsh could signal the arrival of smuggled goods and in turn see a lantern hung from the inn window to tell them all was well. Then it was simply a matter of some of the gang passing the time in gambling and drinking — and more often than not quarrelling — until their comrades in crime arrived with the booty.

One night a quarrel led to a fight and the fight ended with a dead body to dispose of . . . the well at the side of the inn seemed a likely place and perhaps the sounds of cursing and quarrelling and fighting, and the sound of something heavy falling and soon afterwards the sound of footsteps and something being dragged down the stairs and out towards the well is a lasting echo of some tragic and violent happening here long ago.

The well, no longer used, has an odd atmosphere at night and one wonders whether George Ransley, the irritable and hot-tempered leader who was eventually deported for his smuggling activites, returns to the inn he once knew or whether the sounds are those of some other nefarious scoundrel of long ago.

## Bexley

Hall Place is now an educational establishment but the strikingly chequered building once knew grander days. Edward III's eldest son, another Edward but better known as the Black Prince, traditionally because of the dark armour he wore when he so distinguished himself at the Battle of Crécy in 1346, stayed here before departing to fight in the French campaign. Oddly enough the rare appearances here of the ghost of this great and chivalrous military leader are regarded as omens of danger for England or for the occupants of Hall Place.

Wearing his black armour the phantom form has usually been seen at twilight and the appearance is sometimes accompanied by the strains of mediaeval music. Some years ago, when Lady Limerick resided at the Hall, she claimed to have seen the ghost on four occasions and each time it was just before some family trouble or sadness. During the last war the ghost was reportedly seen three times and each time before a British reverse or setback.

Another ghost at Hall Place is that of the Lady Constance, the wife of Sir Thomas Hall, who owned the mansion in the thirteenth century. After he was killed in an accident she was in an agony of despair and threw herself off the tower. Her ghost returns to Hall Place looking for the husband she loved. There is also said to be the ghost of a servant girl in one of the attic bedrooms.

## Bickley

The ghost of Dick Turpin is reputed to haunt the ancient Chequers Inn. They say he often visited this place, using the back stairs when necessary to make a hasty 'disappearance' in a bedroom in the oldest part of the sixteenth century establishment where the long and heavy curtains of a four-poster served as a hiding place.

A barmaid who worked there for over twenty years had no doubt that the 'gentleman in green velvet' that she and others had glimpsed on occasions was in fact the most famous of all highwaymen. A visitor who looked into the empty room some years ago saw a man dressed in green velvet and wearing a hat with a plume in it, sitting at a table writing with a quill pen; but by the time she had related what she had seen and returned to the room, it was deserted. At the time she knew nothing of any reputed ghost at the inn.

Some of the other customers have reported seeing the same figure and also the unexplained forms of ladies in eighteenth century costume, gliding silently along a passage in the upper quarters; and at least one landlord became accustomed to inexplicable ghostly figures, footsteps that had no logical explanation and what sounded like the slamming of doors that were already tightly closed. On many occasions too this landlord, who was at the Chequers for more than a decade, awoke in the middle of the night to find the bed shaking, almost as though there were additional, invisible, occupants. Charles Dickens and Samuel Pepys are among the many distinguished people who have slept here in the past.

The footsteps do seem to have been paranormal in origin. They were often heard apparently emenating from the older rooms in the upper part of the premises and time after time detailed searches revealed no explanation. Once the landlord heard running footsteps and a slamming door and he was convinced that he had cornered the culprit until he found the door that had slammed was bolted on the inside and the room was deserted. Many people have heard and felt odd things at the inn, including temporary and assistant landlords. 'I think there is something peculiar in the place', one landlord said in 1970. 'If there are such things as ghosts, I think there is at least one here . . . '

## Biddenden

The village is best known as the home of Eliza and Mary Chulkhurst, 'the Biddenden Maids', the earliest Siamese twins who lived to adulthood. They are said to have been born in 1100. They were joined together at the hip and shoulder. In 1134 one of the girls died. Doctors proposed to separate the living sister but the survivor refused the operation. 'As we came together, we will go together' she is reported to have said and six hours later she joined her sister in death. In their will the sisters bequeathed twenty acres of land to the parish, providing that the

The Biddenden Maids

rental be used to provide bread and cheese for the poor; and cakes, carrying their images, were to be distributed to strangers in the village each Easter Sunday. For hundreds of years this distribution used to take place in the local church but later the Chulkhurst charity was merged to form a Consolidated Charity. The 'Biddenden cakes', however, are still distributed each Easter and today the village sign commemorates the twins.

Here there has long been reputed to walk the ghost of a love-sick girl, who took her own life and reappears on the anniversary of the event — but unfortunately the date of the tragedy is not known.

That intrepid seeker of ghosts in Kent, Frederick Sanders, heard the story from an elderly Biddenden resident and from the then Rector of Biddenden. The ghost is said to be that of a beautiful young lady, dressed in a magnificent white ball-dress, who is long thought to have haunted the vicinity of a pond in Ibornden Park, the scene of the tragedy.

The story goes that about a century-and-a half ago the local squire and his family were in London for the 'season' when, one evening, they found a baby girl had been left on their doorstep. Failing to trace anyone to whom she belonged and reluctant to put her into an orphanage, they adopted her, gave her the name of Susannah Lost, and brought her up with their only child, a boy. The two children grew up together and in time their childhood affection ripened into love.

On Susannah's eighteen birthday, by which time her loveliness was a legend throughout the Weald, a ball was held in her honour at Ibornden Park. Susannah was the centre of attention, but her young foster-brother, with whom she was passionately in love, seemed to her to ignore her in order to pay attention to a young girl from the neighbouring village of Benenden.

Broken-hearted, Susannah did not have a single dance with her foster-brother, and at midnight she retired to her boudoir, took off her valuable jewellery and flowers, went downstairs, out of the house and then ran across the park towards the pond . . . When she was missed a frantic search was organised and soon they found her body clad in the white ball dress, drowned in the pond in the park. Her ghost, still clad in the white ball-dress, is said to walk round the pond on the anniversary of the tragedy.

As far as Frederick Sanders could establish the drowning of Susannah Lost was probably towards the end of 1837 or possibly early in 1838. A pond is situated a few hundred yards from the mansion in Ibornden Park and is known as Lady Pond.

During the night he spent in the vicinity of Lady Pond with a friend from Rochester, Frederick Sanders neither heard nor saw anything that might be regarded as paranormal and after much research, deliberation and discussion, bearing in mind the fact that the date of the death of Susannah Lost has never been ascertained and that the correct date and time of the tragedy might possibly have brought better results; he felt that she does not haunt the pond. He found the immediate area: the old gardens, the footpath and the drive, all perfectly peaceful and devoid of any psychic unrest; no atmosphere of coldness or depression and in fact the whole place seemed exceptionally peaceful, especially the margins of the allegedly haunted pond.

## Biggin Hill

There are a great many airfields and RAF bases haunted by the ghosts of wartime airmen and their machines. In 1982 a couple of former RAF officers became interested in such reports and discovered a surprising amount of good evidence for apparently paranormal activity on and around airfields and they even succeeded in recording sounds, of aircraft and of people, that they were satisfied had no rational explanation. If such things are possible then surely Biggin Hill, in the very front line during the Battle of Britain and arguably the most famous fighter airfield in the world, is likely to be among the haunted airfields. Indeed it does seem that the ghostly sound of a Spitfire has been heard again at this place.

Those who live around the airfield say there is no mistaking the sound of a Spitfire screaming in to land and it is largely residents and people who know about such things who are the witnesses for these ghostly sounds. The date of 19th January is, I am told, the date when the sounds are most often heard.

Some say the long-dead pilot signals his return with a low Victory roll before coming in to land; others say that mens' voices are heard, glasses clink together and sounds are heard that would have followed the return of a victorious RAF pilot forty years ago. But then, as suddenly and as inexplicably as it began, the sound fades and ceases and Biggin Hill resumes its peaceful atmosphere.

## Bilsington

There are the remains of a thirteenth century priory here, and a stone obelisk to a forgotten politician, Sir William Cosway. Sir William owned the priory and much of the land around but he was killed when he was thrown from a coach at election time; yet his ghost does not walk here but rather, it would seem, some of the inoffensive Augustinian monks who once worshipped here at the monastery founded in 1253 by Sir John Mansell, a priest's son who became Chancellor to Henry III.

Fifty years ago Mr and Mrs Joseph Conrad were out for a drive in their pony and trap, one lovely autumn evening. When they realised that the pony had cast a shoe, they looked for somewhere Mrs Conrad could conveniently rest while her husband went to the nearest forge. Through the gathering dusk they saw they were close to Bilsington Priory, part of which was occupied by a farmer, and they decided to approach the premises.

The farmer's wife readily agreed to allow Mrs Conrad to wait in an adjoining room while her husband attended to the pony and she was shown into a lofty room where a huge and cheerful fire was burning. As the farmer's wife went out of the room to fetch a lamp, Mrs Conrad seated herself comfortably in front of the fire and lightly stroked the head of a friendly wire-haired terrier. Relating what happened next, Mrs Conrad said:

'Suddenly I heard a terrified whimper from the dog. As I gazed at the opposite wall, which seemed to dissolve before my eyes, the room became filled with a choking dust and gritty fog, and through the haze I saw a long procession of habited monks.

'Slowly they passed along a hidden flight of steps, their wooden pattens sounding in ghostly rhythm as they climbed. The return of the farmer's wife with the lamp dispelled the vision or whatever it was I saw; and yet it seemed to verify it for she said: "We can tell the time by the monks' footsteps, six o'clock every evening". The time was exactly six o'clock.'

## Boughton Malherbe

It is many years ago now that Frederick Sanders, local ghost enthusiast and member of the Society for Psychical Research, first told me that the Old Rectory here was haunted by the ghost of a hunch-backed monk in a course grey habit; that the haunted room was in the upper part of the property; that the wife of a former rector saw the ghost inside the house one afternoon, on a bright summer day; and that her daughter saw the same figure one evening.

In an unpublished typescript describing his many investigations at allegedly haunted houses Frederick Sanders says the rambling but picturesque residence dates back to Tudor times and while for generations it had been a rectory, before that, according to his researches, it had been something like a monastery and at one time a manor house. The house, he told me, stood in its own spacious grounds and gardens and was remote from other habitations.

It seems that there are or were several alleged ghosts and hauntings associated with the house but the chief one is the so-called 'Grey Monk' and Frederick Sanders discovered that the first appearance of this figure could have been as early as between 1600 and 1650 and the latest — 'quite recently'.

The wife of the then rector gave the investigator the following account of her sighting of the Grey Monk: 'One afternoon, in June, nearly two years ago, I was adjusting my hat in the bedroom mirror before going out for a walk. It was a glorious day, with the sun shining brilliantly. The bedroom, as you have seen, is at the end of the haunted passage, where it turns left to continue to another part of the house. The door of the bedroom was wide open. From the doorway you can see all the way down the passage, which is some thirty yards in length. The mirror in the room is placed so that the passage can be viewed for the whole of its length in the mirror where it is reflected. While I was putting the finishing touches to my hat I saw a curious figure move silently across the end of the passage, from the stairway leading to the upper parts of the house, and enter the haunted room opposite the stairs.

'It was the figure of the reputed Grey Monk! The shoulders were hunched and the figure was not much over five feet in height. This mysterious apparition — I could not make out the features at the distance — was attired in the habiliments of a monk: long grey dress and grey cowl or hood. I thought it might have been my daughter playing a game and called out to her by name telling her not to creep about so silently as to frighten one, in such a preposterous get-up or disguise. I immediately went along to the haunted room, but found it empty. The figure of the Grey Monk had disappeared. Soon afterwards I ascertained that my daughter was not in fact inside the house at the time, but outside in the front gardens waiting for me to finish dressing and come down to join her.'

The fifteen-year old daughter of the rector then recounted her experience: 'Some months ago I was tidying myself in my room — the door of which leads into the passage — when, happening to glance round towards the door which I

Boughton Malherbe Old Rectory

had left nearly wide open — and without a single thought of ghosts in my mind at the time — I saw the elbow and lower arm and part of the upper arm of some person just out of sight behind the door. The material forming the sleeve was of course cloth — roughish, similar to a tweed — and grey in colour relieved by smallish rusty-like weavings in the grey fabric. The crooked arm moved and vanished. Three strides took me into the passage — nothing was in sight.'

The latter account impressed Frederick Sanders. The rector's wife had seen the mysterious grey figure at a distance of perhaps thirty yards but her daughter had seen the 'grey cloth' part of the figure at a range of only a few feet, six feet at the most. He noted with interest that the 'course tweed-like cloth' described tallied with the rough material used by the austere monks of generations ago for their sombre attire.

In his notes on the case Frederick Sanders records that he was repeatedly informed that the little dog belonging to the wife of the rector could never be induced to cross the threshold of what had become known as the Haunted Room. He also learned that years previously, a former rector of the parish, living at the rectory, was in the habit of giving tramps and vagrants who called at the house for alms, a night's board and lodging in order to test the reputation of the haunted room!

The tramp or passing traveller would be shown into the small room, with its single bed, and invited to rest for the night but it is recorded that none of the 'brotherhood of the road' ever stayed longer than an hour or two, hurriedly leaving the room in a state of terror and making a determined bee-line for the more friendly open highway they had left not long before!

The rector's wife also told Frederick Sanders that 'one day, while in the kitchen, one of the bells connected with the front door rang'. She went immediately to the front of the house, 'but no one was in sight; at the time the house and grounds were completely deserted' (except for herself) 'so who had rung the bell?' She never found the answer and wondered whether there was yet another ghost in the rectory; a ghost that rang bells and interfered with objects.

The rector's daughter recounted to my friend a legend of a very pleasant type of ghost who was said to haunt the house; a ghost known as 'the lady with the flowers'. This ghost had been seen by former owners of the house and the ghost was said to have spoken! She had been reported to walk about the house in a lovely dress of grey silk, and in her right hand she carried a nosegay of flowers. There were stories that she spoke words of comfort to those who had been terrified by the appearance of the Grey Monk and various odd happenings that occurred from time to time. The 'lady with the flowers' usually seemed to say something like, 'Please do not be afraid; I will take care of you!' At one period she always seemed to visit the house on Christmas Eve when she was invariably seen apparently writing letters in the great hall or reading her Bible — but always there was a nosegay of flowers beside her on the desk. Reports of this ghost and of the apparition speaking went back to the nineteenth century but she was also reported during the present century.

Frederick Sanders obtained permission to spend a night alone in the Haunted Room and this he did one cool April night, having had supper at the rectory. His verbatim notes of the event are as follows:

'21.50 Hours: I enter the Haunted Room. It is so well blacked-out that I can see nothing. This room has a small fireplace and a very tiny window. The window is covered by a black cloth. A small door near the window leads out to the bathroom. This door is locked. A small door leads, on the right-hand side of the room into a very small apartment from which there is no other entrance or exit. This door is securely latched. The large door leading into the Haunted Room from the passageway is so built as to exclude all light from the outside. The only article of any description in this room is a plain kitchen chair put there for my convenience. I grope for the chair near the entrance door and sit down. Not a sound. Just a black silence.

'22.00 Hours: The dark silence seems alive — with minute seething "sound". This apparent sensation is only my own blood supply carrying out its normal functions. When one experiences almost one-hundred per cent blackness plus silence the effect is to "crush" the senses: silence can "crush" whereas sound or noise can merely distract.

'22.05 Hours: The room seems colder. I gaze out into the darkness. Suddenly a weird manifestation (presumably of supernormal origin) appears opposite me at the far end of the room. Descending through the dark are streaks and droplets of "something" which glows yellow-green, not unlike liquid-fire. I want to get up from the chair on which I sit, but cannot. The liquid-like fire rolls clean through the darkness and completely vanishes, as if into the wall. This "fire" came from the ceiling and rolled down the wall; about half-way between ceiling and floor it vanished.

'My heart beats a tattoo within me. The blood courses through my veins, but I am cold and shivering. *I have been frightened* — by seeing "something" I had not, even in my wildest hopes, expected to encounter. Still I tried to keep an open mind. The horrible feeling gradually subsided. I found that I could move and rose to my feet, although my legs were unsteady and a general feeling of weakness pervaded the whole of my arms and legs. I decided that these feelings could be ascribed to the action of the sympathetic nervous system and the resultant reaction to the shock or fright.

'The feeling of weakness in the arms and legs though not so "heavy" as that caused by shock induced to the central nervous system by electricity was to a great extent very similar.

'22.08 Hours: Having left the chair I stood still to gain confidence and let the nervous system settle down.

'22.10 Hours: Groped my way over to the far wall. Moved my hand over it. Could see nothing owing to the darkness. Could sense nothing either olfactory or auditory.

'22.15 Hours: Leave room and fetch night light. Examine the walls, floor and ceiling minutely. No evidence to be seen. No sign of phosphorescence. Nothing further happened. First time in my life that I have ever been really frightened.'

Later Frederick Sanders tried to explore his experience and the evidence he had collected in a scientific manner. He felt that seeing the streaks and droplets of something that glowed a yellow-green colour had been such a sudden shock to his nervous system that momentarily he had been paralysed as far as movement was concerned although he was fully conscious as to his surroundings and the phenomena he was witnessing. He felt glued to the chair he was sitting in although he wished to rise; his heart beats increased; the circulation of his blood became faster and more physically apparent. Then he became very cold and began to shiver. He had unquestionably been frightened and the horrible feeling gradually subsided as the para-sympathetic system became normal after the swift reaction caused by the sympathetic system. A feeling of weakness had been apparent for some time afterwards in his arms but not, he thought, as weak a feeling as would have been imparted by a sudden electrical shock to the nervous system.

A few months after his visit to Boughton Malherbe Rectory Frederick Sanders wrote to the rector and requested permission to spend a whole night in the Haunted Room, when he planned to take temperature readings, photographic recordings and 'attempt to gather impressions with the aid of very fine powder'. The rector was agreeable to a further investigation but not for the time being. Later Frederick Sanders tried again, twice, during the succeeding six years but he received no reply to these communications.

He explained to me the circumstances in which the strange experience took place; agreeing with me that it was a great pity that he had no co-watcher with him in the room on that occasion who could have verified the phenomena he experienced. He said: 'I have no doubt that the lights were illusionary, to this extent: that they sprang from a known cause and the causation was the emittance of rays of light, not from the wall, but by light falling upon the surface of the wall. It was certainly not hallucinatory.

'In the Haunted Room there are three doors. One upon the long passageway extending from practically end to end of the breadth of the house on the first storey. One leading out of the room in the vicinity of the farther left-hand corner. The other door gives access mid-way along the right-hand wall to a very small room. On the left-hand side of the opposite wall to the wall abutting on the long passage or upstairs corridor is a very small window hardly large enough to allow a person to squeeze through and below the window (which is at the back of the rectory) there is a sheer drop.

'When I went to the rectory I naturally put all of its inhabitants above practical joking. Therefore I did not seal the three doors, but only tested them to see that they were securely closed. The window was blacked-out owing to war-time precautions. The room was — with the exception of a plain kitchen chair — absolutely bare, floor, walls and ceiling.

'I might add that while at supper with the rector and his family the rector's young son made one or two tentative attempts at "tapping" with his foot against his chair. The rector mildly remonstrated with him and the "taps" ceased. Also, the rector told me that he was going to retire early as he had a heavy Sunday ahead of him. His son was to retire also and was not to sit up. The rector's wife and daughter would await the end of the investigation and see me on my way at the completion of the investigation. All these arrangements were, of course, quite in order.

'While I was in the Haunted Room I heard the rector and his son ascend the stairs to the long corridor. They were both talking. After this I did not hear anything more. I carried out my watch uninterrupted excepting for the unusual appearance of the dropping or falling "drops" of yellow-green light on the farther wall of the haunted chamber.

'I took nothing into the room except my luminous watch. This I kept in the breast pocket of my jacket. After the lights had vanished and I was sufficiently recovered from the shock of this manifestation of light in the room in which, owing to exceptional darkness, I could not even see my own hand in front of my face, I tried the door leading into the room from the corridor and it was shut; I did not open it. I felt my way along the right-hand wall to the door leading into the small room and this too was shut fast; I did not open this door. Feeling my way along the wall I felt round until I came to the wall farthest from the corridor and moved my hands over the surface of the wall where the lights had appeared above the fireplace. Continuing, I came to the blacked-out window, and ascertained that the fittings were intact. I continued round to the left-hand wall and found the third door secure; this door I did not open. Then I moved round until I came back to the chair from which I had begun my tour of inspection. I then moved across from point to point in the room. I encountered nothing. Then I opened the door and stepped out into the passage. The rector had left a dim light burning about half-way down the passage. I walked to the opposite end of the passage to where a tiny night-light lamp stood upon a small table. With this I returned to the room and carried out a thorough inspection of floor, walls, ceiling, fire-place and doors. Nothing was amiss. The area of wall above the fire-place where the dropping lights had appeared was absolutely devoid of marks or moisture or anything of a chemical nature.

'After fully investigating the room I returned the night-lamp to its former position and went downstairs. I told the rector's wife about the falling "drops of light" and she vouchsafed no comment upon this apparent phenomena. Very shortly afterwards I left the rectory.

'Ruling out the theory of the lights being illusory or hallucinatory I can only conjecture upon the phenomena — but light got into that room somehow! How did it gain admittance? The light beams must have been very narrow not to have been seen in the very well darkened room. Could such a phenomenon be caused by apparatus directed by a person in such a manner as to cause a "materialisation" without the person and the apparatus being detected? To this the answer must be: yes.

'By means of experiments in my own home I was able to produce similar "phenomena" with apparatus directed by myself in a darkened room without my presence being known and without showing the emittance of beams of light.

'The apparatus I used consisted of a battery cycle lamp with the reflector reversed over the light bulb and thus cutting the light beam down to a minimum of size. The front of the lamp was then boxed-off and rendered so as not to emit any light until required. A slide (vertical) was then fixed to the boxed-off front part of the lamp at a distance from the aperature of the reversed reflector. The distance necessary to obtain the best results I obtained by experimentation. The lower third of the slide was blacked out; the middle third was also blacked-out with the exception of pear-shaped spaces, arranged in order to break up the beam of light into smaller beams; and the top third of the slide was blacked-out.

'With this simple apparatus I was able to carefully open a door leading into a blacked-out room and enter in stockinged feet without being detected. I had the light on in the apparatus. By focussing on a pre-determined part of the wall not far from the doorway, I was able to produce "falling lights or drops" by gently lowering the slide down and so passing the middle-third over the light beam where it was broken up by the clear pear-shaped spaces. The top third then cut off all light and the "lights" ceased. The same effect was procured by this apparatus as was witnessed in the Haunted Room at the rectory. This leaves the question of paranormal activity open to full conjecture. Were the Haunted Room "lights" of supernormal origin? Were they semi-illusory as made by artificial light finding its way accidentally into the room? Or were they deliberately manufactured?'

In May 1984, I visited the Old Rectory and my wife and I and our friends Freda and Steuart Kiernander were shown over the rambling but beautiful old house that is now the home of Mrs Keen. We visited the Haunted Room and the adjoining small room; the bedroom where the rector's wife had seen the ghost in the mirror; the haunted passageway; the great hall; the kitchen and the gardens. Mrs Keen sleeps in the room where the ghost was mirrored and here, she told us, the wife of a former rector is said to have jumped to her death from a window. A ghost has been said to manifest here, looking over the shoulder of people who are looking into the mirror; but Mrs Keen told us that the only part of the undoubtedly atmospheric house that she feels may still be haunted is the end of the upstairs passageway (where the Grey Monk is supposed to have appeared), near the top of the stairway where, as she places her hand on the corner wall, she often has the impression that another hand is about to be placed over hers . . .

I found the corridor or passageway full of atmosphere and could well imagine spectral figures being seen there in days gone by. The little room that used to be called the Haunted Room seemed full of light and happiness. The lovely garden brooded quietly in the May sunshine and the old house slumbered with a gentle undercurrent of 'something' appropriate to its years and to its chequered history.

## Bridge

Among the curiosities to be seen at the old Norman church here is a weird sculpture of a snake crawling through the eye of a skull; distinctly odd scenes of the garden of Eden, one showing the devil climbing up a tree in the guise of a strange bird; and, in a recess in the wall, the stone figure of a priest in his robes: Macobus Kasey, the vicar here in the early 1500s.

There is, or was, a country club housed in a delightful seventeenth century building where the owner awakened one morning, a few months after he had purchased the property, to see the figure of a serving maid, dressed in old-fashioned clothes, walking silently across his bedroom from one wall to the other, carrying a linen basket which she placed gently on the floor. She turned towards him and then vanished, as did the basket.

Later some of the club members enquired about a 'young woman in old-fashioned clothing' whom they said they had seen standing at the top of a flight of stairs.

Andrew Green says there is a story associated with the building that tells of the then owner fathering a child by a serving maid and of the murdered child's body being hidden somewhere in the house (? in a linen basket). The sound of a baby sobbing pitifully has been reported, apparently emanating from the vicinity of a chimney on the ground floor.

# Canterbury

With its magnificent walls, old gateways, fine old gabled houses, stone carvings that Chaucer may have looked at and the endless glories of its cathedral, small wonder that Canterbury is as much a place of pilgrimage today as ever it was and the atmosphere in the north-west transept, site of the murder of Thomas Becket, is apparent to many people.

Simon of Sudbury, Archbishop of Canterbury, Lord Chancellor, was murdered here in 1381 by followers of Wat Tyler, who displayed the head on London Bridge for six days. Then it went to St Gregory's Church, Sudbury in Suffolk, where it has been preserved ever since. Some years ago the bell-ringers there were disturbed by mysterious footsteps and other unexplained sounds, which they put down to the ghostly perambulations of Simon of Sudbury, but his ghost has more frequently been reported to haunt the tower that bears his name at Canterbury; and a possible reason might be that his head and his body were never reunited; yet the figure that is thought to be the ghost of Simon of Sudbury is no headless ghost but a tall and dignified man with a grey beard and a fresh complexion.

Eighty-year-old Charles Denne told me that he had dwelled there with a ghost for over twenty years. It all began when he retired one evening to his bedroom at the top of the Sudbury Tower, where he lived all alone. After a busy day repairing shoes, he was having a rest before getting himself an evening meal when he heard someone knocking at his bedroom door; there were three distinct knocks and then the door opened.

Although he knew that he was alone on the premises, Mr Denne told me that he did not feel afraid as he saw that his late visitor, apparently as solid and substantial as himself, although wearing very out-of-date clothes and what looked like a grey robe, walk slowly towards his bed. Mr Denne said that he felt a strong feeling of friendliness emanating from the stranger and as he rose from his bed to offer the visitor his hand in welcome, the strange figure with its grey square-cut beard, bowed three times — and disappeared.

Mr Denne never saw the figure again but he often felt the presence in his bedroom and on occasions he was aware of a pair of hands 'tucking him in' at night-time. He often heard strange tapping noises which sometimes came before he had the feeling that his 'visitor' was in the room with him.

An ominously-named entrance within the precincts of the cathedral, the Dark Entry, is reputedly haunted by the ghost of Nell Cook. Richard Barham, who was born in Canterbury, recounts the story in his *Ingoldsby Legends*. It seems that Nell was so shocked at finding her master, a cathedral canon, in compromising circumstances with a young lady, that she poisoned them both. The body of the murderess was eventually buried beneath the paving stones of the Dark Entry, which she haunts, especially, according to reports, on Friday nights.

Soon after my volume *Hauntings* was published in 1977 I received a letter from Mr C.J. Fleetney of Canterbury. He describes himself as a 'poor man's parson', involved with the cathedral and the Anglican Church in and around Canterbury and he has assisted with services in the Cathedral Church. The account that he sent to me is, he says, 'as far as I am concerned perfectly true'. I quote from Mr Fleetney's letter verbatim:

'As a trainee Reader, Lay-Minister of the Church of England, shortly to be admitted to the Office, I was expected to attend a series of lectures on ministering to the dying. The venue was the Chapel of Our Lady Undercroft, in the crypt of Canterbury Cathedral.

'The evening of Thursday, 19th October 1976, was dark. The clouds were low and racing across the sky from the south-west, driven by a gale that was fast stripping the last of the autumn leaves from the trees. My wife and I parked our car some way from the cathedral, and leaned into the wind and bitter rain as we made our way along St Margaret's Street, across St Peter's Street, and through narrow Mercery Lane towards Christ Church Gate. There were few people about and, it seemed, no vehicles, and the only noise was the booming of the gale, the creaking of the swinging signs above shop fronts, and the hiss of the rain on the pavements. The cathedral, vast and grey, towered above us into the blackness of the night. The south porch, the main entrance, was closed and gated, and not a trace of light glimmered from the nave windows. In company with other people we made our way across the wet turf to the tiny, narrow door set in the wall of the south-west transept.

'One or two small electric lights threw vague shadows among the tattered battle flags stirring in the wind, in St Michael's Chapel. The great building stretched away in deep shadow, hinting at enormous height and space. High above us, in the fan vaulting of the central tower, the gale boomed and muttered. We followed a verger down, under the south aisle of the choir, to the crypt.

'Part of the Chapel of Our Lady Undercroft is frequently used as a lecture hall, the low-pitched nave, and the lecturer uses a lectern in a central position, with his back to the altar. The entire chapel is on one level; there are no steps to chancel or sanctuary. It is the oldest part of the cathedral, having survived the fires that destroyed the building above during the early Middle Ages. The chapel is not an ideal lecture hall as it is necessarily cluttered by short heavy Norman columns which support the tremendous weight above.

'The chapel was well-lighted and warm, comfortably full, but we managed to find seats in the centre but to the right of the speaker. A verger sat at the controls of the public address system and those of us who were students settled down with pen and pad to take notes as the lecture progressed, while the greater number, my wife included, enjoyed listening to this man, well-known in his particular field.

'Beyond the lecturer the chancel and sanctuary was in semi-darkness illuminated only by the light from the main body of the chapel. From where we were sitting the altar was obscured by a column, and when I glanced up from my notes, my view beyond the lecturer was the curving blind arcading of the wall between the altar and the corner of the organ which in turn obscured my view to the extreme left. Above the wall's blind arcading the narrow lancets soared up to break ground level. They were clear glass and the gale caused the shadows of bare branches to toss and flicker across the lattice-work.

'Some ten minutes before the mid-lecture break I was aware of a flicker of movement against the blind arcading, some thirty feet from where I was sitting. I glanced quickly from my notes and saw the movement again. I realised that I had caught a brief glimpse of a verger moving from left to right: that is, from the point where the corner of the organ blocked my view, towards the altar, masked by the column close to my chair. Once again, just before the lecturer closed the first part of his talk, I caught this flicker of movement as the figure moved along the arcading towards the altar.

'The recess lasted some ten minutes and as question time was to follow people were scribbling notes on small squares of paper given out for the purpose. I asked my wife whether she had noticed the verger moving about, beyond the lecturer. She said that she had noticed some kind of movement, but not at pavement level, rather higher up, near the windows. While we spoke she drew my attention suddenly to a movement. Together we agreed that in fact she could see the shadows of the wind-tossed branches, and perhaps the shadows of people walking round the Corona towards the King's School. I suggested that in point of fact it was a poor time to prepare the altar for the next day's services, as the constant movement was, to say the least, disturbing when one was feverishly taking notes.

'The lecturer called us to order and question time began. I kept my eyes half trained on the distant wall at first but quickly became immersed in the discussion. Then, suddenly, there he was again! Moving towards the altar, close to the arcading. I turned to my notes, mildly annoyed. A few minutes later, due to a remark by the lecturer, I glanced up and experienced an indescribable and overwhelming fear that welled up inside me and I saw the figure move in a ghastly kind of puppet-like motion from right to left, along the arcading, and then vanish behind the organ. In that instant I somehow knew that the cassocked figure I was seeing was somehow unreal. I waited for it to return, left to right, but true to form it did not appear while I waited, and before I could relax and turn my attention to the lecturer, the session ended.

'The lecture was followed by tea and cakes. We milled round and people formed small groups to discuss the theme of the evening. I waited my opportunity and waylaid the busy verger.

' "Were you busy preparing vestments for tomorrow's services just now?" I asked. "I've been at the public address console all evening, Sir, why?" He was attempting to edge past me anxious to get things cleared away, for it was late and no doubt he had a full day facing him on the Friday. "Oh, I thought I saw you or one of your colleagues . . . " I saw him searching my face. "I'm the only verger on duty tonight, but you thought you saw someone over by the far wall?" He pointed towards the far wall between the altar and the organ. I nodded and the verger eased me to one side and smiled.

' "I'm the only verger here tonight, Sir," he repeated. "Now, if you'll excuse me". It was quite obvious that he had no intention of discussing something that he knew well enough I had seen.

'I did not question anyone else that evening. I ought to have done, but things drifted on and we broke up and went our separate ways. Several days later I mentioned the incident to one of the Cathedral guides. She considered for a moment but said that apart from the well-known "Becket's Shadow" which can be seen on one of the crypt columns, she knew of no other "ghost" in the Undercroft.

'The facts are that at no time did I see the figure when I actually watched for it. It only appeared when I became involved with my notes and glanced up, briefly. At first it was just a flicker of black against the stone of the arcading. Later it seemed to be a thin person of medium height wearing a cassock. I do not recall head or hands, just a cassock, drifting along in a busy, purposeful manner. It was not until I saw it move from right to left that I realised I had seen it move, perhaps five times, always from left to right. Only on the last occasion did its behaviour strike me as somehow horrible and extremely frightening; only then did it strike me that it might be other than a verger . . . '

The ghost of Thomas Becket was reportedly seen a few years ago, near one of the pillars in the crypt, 'distinct and unmistakable'; and I have another report of a shadowy figure that could not be explained, being seen by a group of visitors to the Cathedral. At first they thought someone must be rehearsing for a play or tableau of some kind for the costume was unmistakably of olden days but they discovered, on enquiry, that such was not the case and the figure disappeared in circumstances that were quite inexplicable.

One of the Cathedral staff was very interested in the experiences of this group and told them that he had heard about a similar sighting a few months earlier. The atmosphere and overwhelming sense of history and tragedy that pervades Canterbury Cathedral could well influence certain individuals, but could it account for a figure seen by two different groups of people on two different occasions?

In 1929 Mrs Anne Chesshyre was helping in the stables at a manor house near Canterbury when she was surprised to hear the sound of horses' hooves galloping towards the stables across the cobbled yard. The family dog heard the sounds too and dashed out to meet them, barking furiously. Thinking that the barking dog would further frighten any horses that had escaped from the ponies' field, Anne hurried out to find nothing to account for the loud and distinct sounds. She then ascertained that the ponies were all quietly grazing in their field and relieved but very puzzled she returned to her work in the stables.

A few moments later she again heard the sound of wild galloping and this time the dog cowered in the corner of the stable, obviously terrified by the sounds. Again Anne hurried out to see what was going on and again she was met with complete silence and no explanation for the sounds.

Later, she learned that what she had experienced constituted the Manor House ghost story. Many years earlier a pair of horses had bolted, turning their carriage over and killing some of the occupants. At intervals ever since, and approximately at the same time of the year as the accident had happened, the sound of galloping horses' hooves had, she was told, often been heard.

In November 1982 Miss Joyce Sewell of Honiton was good enough to write to me, saying, 'I am wondering if you may have heard of the ghost of a monk that used to haunt one of the houses in Burgate, Canterbury, owned by the Ecclesiastical Commissioners?

'A Mrs Findlay (now deceased), whom I knew, used to live there and she told others and myself that she had seen this ghost — who seemed of a melancholy disposition — twelve times! He always held one of his arms in a crooked position.

'During the course of some digging that took place in the precincts of the Cathedral a skeleton was unearthed with one arm in this same crooked position. The remains were given Christian burial and Mrs Findlay said that the next time she saw "her ghost" he was cheerful and singing happily!

'I might add that this took place on the third floor of the house and the Head Verger at the Cathedral knew all about this ghost at the time . . . '

## Chartham

A delightful village gathered round its green with a charming peep of Canterbury Cathedral four miles away. Howfield Manor, standing on old monastic land, has the ghost of a monk, according to Joan Forman.

The ancient story is one of death during bravery. It is said that when the monastery was destroyed by fire a kindly and brave monk, with no thought of his own safety, died in an effort to rescue one of his brethren from the engulfing flames; his considerable exertions saved the life of the apparently doomed brother, but the rescuer died from the injuries he received and it is his ghost that has long been said to walk here.

At Howfield Manor, which may occupy the actual site of the vanished monastery, the sound of chanting voices has been heard on many occasions; a psychic echo perhaps of the thousands of times the monks must have practised their devotions on this spot, permeating the atmosphere and reproducing those sounds of long ago on rare occasions when the required conditions are fulfilled.

# Chatham

There are several ghost stories associated with the famous naval barracks and if today the bustling, busy town seems singularly unhaunted, listen to Samuel Pepys, writing about his official visit to the dockyard in 1661:

'Then to the Hill House at Chatham, where I never was before, and I found a pretty pleasant house, and am pleased with the armes that hang up there. Here we supped very merry, and late to bed; Sir William telling me that old Edgebarrow, his predecessor, did die and walk in my chamber, did make me somewhat afraid, but not so much as for mirth's sake I did seem. So to bed in the Treasurer's chamber. Lay and slept till three in the morning, and then waking and by the light of the moon I saw my pillow (which overnight I flung from me) stand upright, but not bethinking myself what it might be I was a little afraid, but sleep overcome all, and so lay till nigh morning, at which time I had a candle brought me, and a good fire made, and in general it was a great pleasure all the time I staid here to see how I am respected and honoured by all people . . . '

St Mary's Barracks have long been said to be haunted by the sound of limping footsteps and the tapping of a crutch or wooden leg and it is thought that these ghostly sounds must be a legacy of some forgotten visit to the barracks by a wounded ex-serviceman who was mistakenly shot as an intruder. The sounds have most frequently been reported during the Middle Watch, midnight to four a.m. when, it might be thought, the night is at its darkest, shadows can easily assume physical forms and mistakes can easily happen.

Nevertheless this ghost has acquired a name: Peg-leg Jack; his stumping ground is towards Room 34 of Cumberland Block, the oldest part of the barracks; and at least one sighting is officially on record in the duty officer's log book: 'Ghost reported seen during Middle Watch'.

Antony Coxe has said that two adjoining houses in Magpie Hall Road have been haunted for more than twenty years, but a psychical researcher friend, who lives in Chatham, tells me he has no convincing evidence.

A building that has seen life as a cinema, a hostel and temporary shelter for people bombed out of their homes, and a bingo hall has, according to reports, been periodically haunted for upwards of forty years.

During the Second World War, when the Church Army had charge of the premises and used it as a hostel, a nearby bomb caused many casualties of varying degrees of seriousness with four people being killed, three of them children.

Within months there were stories of 'strange noises' occurring in the building, usually at night-time (when the bombing had occurred), noises that sent chills up the spines of those who heard them for, to all intents and purposes, another bomb had fallen and again there was panic and screams of the injured and dying . . .

Some years later reports of similar sounds were still being circulated although the sounds had reduced in volume and those who heard them variously described them as 'muffled thuds', 'faint screams' and 'cries that seemed to come from a distance'. But with the lessening of the volume of sound a visual form began to appear in reports, usually described as a man in rather out-of-date clothes who was sometimes seen for a moment in the foyer area or upstairs on the balcony. Some of the witnesses said the man's suit seemed to be a dull shade of green, possibly a military uniform, and so the ghostly figure acquired the appellation of 'the man in green'.

This figure, like the ghostly sounds, favoured the hours after daylight and was in fact most frequently seen during the evening. One night worker, a cleaner, said he saw the figure several times but on each occasion he only just managed to catch a glimpse of it and then, almost before it had registered, it had gone. This witness also stated that on occasions, and certainly more than once, he had distinctly heard the sound of childrens' voices. He was positive that these sounds originated from within the building but he was never really able to pinpoint exactly where they came from.

After he had made an official report concerning the sounds he could not account for, he discovered that other staff members of the establishment had also heard the sound of childrens' voices and two said they were certain they had seen a man in a green military-style suit, a man who disappeared in circumstances which caused them to believe that they had seen a ghost.

Some ten years ago a sensitive spent some time inside the property and said that she repeatedly heard the name 'Bill Malan' clairvoyantly. She said she thought he was associated with the building when it had been a cinema and that he was 'the man in green'. Subsequently it was discovered that a William Malan had indeed been employed as a commissionaire at the cinema for many years and he was known for his concern for the safety and welfare of children. He died in 1955 but it was remembered that he always wore a green uniform when on duty at the cinema.

One wonders whether his deep concern, the traumatic bombing, the fear and panic, and the injury, pain and death associated with the building may have all somehow combined to contribute to an occasional recurrence of some of the happenings here in years past.

## Cheriton

The nineteenth century mansion here known as Underhill House once belonged to the Brockmans of Beachborough. Here, if we are to believe varied reports, there have been a murder and at least three suicides and a history of ghosts and hauntings and mysterious events that caused the Army-owned property to stand empty for years and to become derelict. Eventually the mansion was extensively damaged by fire.

Mr G.B. Boreham, Reference Librarian at Folkestone, tells me that they have in their files an obituary of Alured Denne who, though it is not stated clearly, appears to have committed suicide at Underhill House in 1887.

Here, in 1913, when the property was used as Brigade Headquarters, a young Army officer, faced with huge gambling debts, shot himself in the entrance hall. In 1932 an officer's servant had an affair with a housemaid that ended in the batman, in a fit of rage, cutting the girl's throat on her own bed; and rather than face the consequences, in the cold light of day the next morning, he shot himself in the narrow stairway leading to the kitchen, just as the police broke in to arrest him. Some years later an Army padre hanged himself in the airing cupboard off the main corridor.

Among the allegedly ghostly happenings there is the phantom form of a soldier seen by two girls sleeping in one of the bedrooms — they said it emerged out of the wall and glided across the room; footsteps in the passageway adjoining the airing cupboard, heard by cleaning personnel when there was no other living person in the house; the ghost form of a young woman reportedly seen on several occasions in the bedroom where a young woman was murdered; and a string of odd incidents that occurred when Underhill House was used as a hostel for students.

Once a laundry basket inexplicably found its way into the locked house and a few hours later completely disappeared from the locked house. This incident was vouched for by two witnesses, ladies who let themselves into the house in the morning, saw the laundry basket and told themselves they would move it later in the day. When they returned in the afternoon it had disappeared. At the time no one else had the keys of the property, only the Colonel's daughter and her companion: the two witnesses for this occurrence.

Ten years ago three people visited the house, which was then standing empty, and having explored every room in the house, they were about to leave when an electric light bulb dropped to the floor behind them — not only were they surprised that this should happen but they were astonished to find that it had not broken when it fell on to the hard wooden floor.

Other incidents have included the displacement of cutlery and other objects in the dining-room; a disembodied voice heard in the kitchen; a clammy coldness in certain 'haunted' areas, even on the warmest day; and a brooding, resentful feeling that has affected many people for no apparent reason.

Once, a housekeeper caught a glimpse of 'an old man in a pepper-and-salt suit' in a doorway leading to the cellars. The wine cellars are thought to have led into a subterranean passage in which, during the Civil War, James Stuart, Duke of Richmond, used to hide while waiting to cross the Channel with messages to the later Charles II. Some sources state that the passage led to a wood or coppice, later known as Richmond's Shave. What is certain is that the Victorian Underhill House, extensively damaged by fire in 1978, was built on the site of a much earlier building and, as at famous Borley Rectory 'the most haunted house in England', the building of a house where murder and suicide took place, on the site of another building where equally tragic happenings occurred, may have caused a vortex of emotions that exploded into psychic disturbances.

## Chilham

The Square here has been described as a piece of Old England at her very best and certainly the place is steeped in history and very lovely. Here Julius Caesar had one of his early conflicts with the Britons, possibly his very first battle in this country.

The ghost of the Rev Sampson Hieron, who knew Chilham when he was vicar in the seventeenth century, is generally accepted as haunting the inglenook of the picturesque White Horse Inn. When I was there I asked why the vicar should haunt the public house in the village square rather than perhaps the church or churchyard and I learned that before the place became an inn, and a delightful and excellent one at that, it was Vicar Hieron's home. Even today there is a lot of evidence for the sudden appearance and equally sudden disappearance of the shadowy form of a grey-haired old man, in black gown and gaiters, standing gazing into the fire with his hands behind his back; remembering perhaps some troubled time in his life at Chilham.

He died in 1677 and lies buried in the churchyard of St Mary's Church but before he reached that final resting place (?) he was evicted from the living of Chilham for his nonconformist views . . . and now his ghost returns, usually at ten minutes past ten in the morning (notwithstanding summer time or even double summer time) and should an unsuspecting customer bid the kindly-looking old gentleman, who sometimes sits in a chair beside the fireplace, 'Good day'; the phantom figure of Sampson Hieron promptly vanishes!

King John stayed at Chilham and enjoyed hunting the black fallow deer which still roam the estate. The present Chilham Castle was completed by Sir Dudley Digges in the year that Shakespeare died and today it is the seat of Viscount Massereene and Ferrard.

At the old Jacobean castle there is reputed to walk the ghost of a mediaeval lady. She was last seen a few years ago during a mediaeval banquet and the person seeing her, taking her for a real person, prepared to approach and greet her, whereupon the phantom form that a second earlier had looked so real and solid and life-like, simply melted into the wall and disappeared.

In the kitchen area mysterious tapping sounds have been reported from time to time, always apparently emanating from one particular part of a wall. Since the walls here are some ten feet thick one suspects a hidden room or secret apartment and indeed there are stories of a lady being bricked-up here long ago; a lady whose ghost haunted this ancient and atmospheric building up to Victorian times. Now perhaps all that remains of this ghost are the sounds of heavy furniture being dragged about and an unnatural coldness in a so-called

Chilham Castle

'haunted room'. Investigator of the paranormal Andrew Green has said that he heard the sounds and noticed a 'severe' drop in temperature during a visit to Chilham Castle in 1975.

When I asked the present Viscount Massereene and Ferrard about any ghostly associations at Chilham Castle, his private home, he told me: 'We do "ghost tours" in the Keep, all that remains of the Norman castle, but there is no particular single ghost as far as I know although one or two people have claimed to have seen apparitions, the last being a maid who fell down the stairs and broke her leg because she claimed she saw a ghost. There have certainly been many remains of Roman soldiers and others excavated on the site.

'Regarding the Jacobean castle, it is reported to have the usual Grey Lady wandering up and down the stairs, but the house has a very un-ghostly atmosphere and I have never seen anything myself. I have seen ghosts as a child, at my father's seat in Ireland, Antrim Castle, but not here.'

## Cliffe north of Rochester

A haunting associated with the Black Bull Inn at Cliffe may be the result of the place being built on the site of an old graveyard — so runs the local story; and when Dickens wandered about this lovely and evocative part of the county, the property was an attractive, weather-boarded cottage and the ghostly hulks of abandoned prison ships littered Cliffe Marshes.

The inn is supposed to have occupied the site of a demolished church and then, it is thought, all might have been well but graveyards are popularly supposed to be haunted places and if the inn stands on a graveyard — well, may that not be the reason that ghostly footsteps and other nocturnal sounds have been known to disturb occupants and visitors alike? And who but a ghost could repeatedly open a securely fastened door upstairs, a door that opens on to the passage and bedrooms where the sound of footsteps has been heard when no human being could have been responsible?

## Cooling

Little remains of Cooling's fourteenth century castle, once the home of Sir John Oldcastle, Shakespeare's 'the good Lord Cobham' and the scene of a short and inglorious seige of six hours during Wyatt's rebellion; today the place is best remembered as Pip's village in *Great Expectations*, and Dickens used the thirteen round gravestones in the churchyard as the row of graves in which Pip's brothers and sisters lay.

Certainly Charles Dickens often walked in this very weird churchyard and many people believe that some psychic element of the great novelist still lingers at the place that acted on Dickens like a magnet. Here he would spend hours lost in his own imagination and there is no denying an unusual atmosphere, quiet and brooding, and not a little mysterious, that could well be conducive to psychic happenings. Frederick Sanders, a great lover of Dickens and no mean psychic investigator, told me he found it the most impressive place he had ever visited, from a psychic point of view.

One night in mid-December he and his wife spent some hours there and Sanders himself had an experience which he was never able to completely explain in rational terms. They entered by the west gate into the churchyard and almost immediately they both saw a shaft of pale silver light shining at a small window high up in the square tower of the church; it did not move or flicker for several seconds, then it faded and disappeared, only to suddenly reappear a few seconds later. Sanders decided that the light was in fact a reflection of the moon, the disappearance and reappearance being caused by the moon becoming momentarily obscured by a cloud.

After exploring the church, which they found 'uncannily silent and ghostly in the soft moonlight that streamed through the windows' they moved out into the porch where Frederick Sanders' wife sat on a seat inside the porch while he decided to settle himself near an old yew tree about halfway along the south side of the church. Just as he was about to leave his wife she said she could hear movements from the direction of the churchyard and looking in the direction she indicated they both saw the top half of a moonlit figure moving (or rather gliding) at a very swift pace just beyond a low wall that flanked the south side of the churchyard.

Within seconds it had disappeared from sight but Sanders hurried over to the wall and looked in the direction in which the figure had disappeared — and he quickly solved the mystery. A cyclist was just disappearing from view after having ridden along a rough track bordering the field near the south wall and he was responsible for the 'gliding figure' they had seen!

After spending some time near the old yew tree with nothing to report other than an owl out hunting and an occasional bat squeaking nearby, Sanders returned to keep his wife company in the church porch. After a while Frederick Sanders said he would like to spend a little while alone in the church and his wife said she would remain where she was.

Once inside the church Sanders quietly concentrated on Dickens and what might have happened in this old country church and churchyard a hundred years earlier. After some fifteen minutes of mental concentration the present seemed to slip away and in some curious fashion the past seemed to be reconstructed within his mind. I quote from his report of the experience:

'I stood a few feet within the church from the closed main entrance door from the porch. I buttoned my overcoat collar up for it was very cold, thrust my hands deep into the pockets, closed my eyes and tried to blank out my mind from all thought as far as I was able to do so.

'Minutes passed, minutes of silence and frustration; and then, suddenly, I conceived a mental picture of Cooling church and churchyard, as viewed from the south-western corner of the churchyard. The time of year seemed to be summer for the sun was shining brightly, it was hot, and the time of day seemed to be mid-afternoon.

'A few seconds later greyish-shadow-forms of people, like pale silhouette figures, moved about over near the church porch. There was a general haziness but I could distinguish high hats, bonnets, long jackets and large-skirted dresses associated with the forms. The general impression of the period conveyed by the clothing would seem to be anywhere around the 1840-1860 era.

'These indistinct figures then faded out, but one remained, and it was a very conspicuous figure which seemed to grow clearer and clearer as the mental image of the shape built up, association by association, until I felt I could have touched it.

'The figure was that of a woman and as the figure took shape and stood there, I saw, with her back to me, a female dressed in a silk bonnet and a dress with voluminous hooped skirt and lovely frills. The silk bonnet was of a pearly sheen, as was the beautiful dress with its deep frills of exquisite dark blue.

'In her right hand she carried what appeared to be a silk parasol and, blazing from a gold ring upon a finger of her left hand, a fine solitaire diamond. Suddenly she half-turned her head and the sun caught the golden curls beneath the bonnet. Out of her plump and happy face with its delicate pink complexion, a pair of laughing blue eyes shone and sparkled. Her mouth, humorous and generously shaped, laughed in tune with the look in her eyes.

'All at once the young woman swung round and ran some yards from the porch as though to meet someone. A man emerged into the sunlight of the churchyard and the lady of the pearly silk dress ran towards the south-east section of the churchyard where there is a small gateway in the corner. The man advanced towards the smiling lady.

'He was dressed in a black stove-pipe hat and a frock-coat, also of black. His trousers are of a peat-and-heather mixture in colour, and the cloth seems to be made up of a medium-sized check patterning. Shining black boots of soft leather fitted his feet like gloves. In his right hand he carried a gold-topped walking stick of highly polished dark-brown wood. His height was about five feet nine inches and he had a military bearing. I seemed to hear him call to the woman although there was no real sound or speech.

'She laughed and ran a few steps farther away and then turned, waving her left hand, and turned away again, to run quickly out of sight beyond the churchyard, along the old field path behind the back gardens of the row of cottages near the east side of the church. The man stopped walking and stood still, pondering it seemed, what to do next.

'Then the man turned round and came towards me; as he neared the west wall of the churchyard I could see that he sported a medium beard of soft light brown hair but I could not see any features! It was a shock and rather frightening for behind the blank fleshy mask I somehow knew that emotions were trying to compose the features of this figure and I even thought I could make out a skin-deep contortional movement, like ripples moving in various directions over a blank surface . . .

'I tried to hold my attention on the blank surface of where there should have been a face and the skin movements continued but nothing I could do would hold the scene and the pictures ended with the featureless face.'

Looking back on the experience Frederick Sanders told me that it really was a very strange and curious experience and although he had at first consciously tried to produce something, as the scene continued it seemed to be completely out of his control and he simply watched, until he encountered the faceless man and, by hindsight, he wondered whether this 'facelessness' could have been caused by the honesty of his own consciousness and thought in refusing to give way to imagination and so fitting the *features of Charles Dickens* to the figure. The struggle between truth and imaginative force might, he felt, cause the blank features and the apparent agitation of it.

In spite of extensive enquiries Frederick Sanders was not able to unearth any evidence of an affair-of-the-heart between Dickens and some unknown female, to which the psychic scene would seem to point — at Cooling, but he was still faced by the peculiar attraction this rural spot had for the novelist; an attraction that some visitors have themselves felt to such an extent that they have almost seen and felt the presence of Dickens, as did Frederick Sanders on that unforgettable December night.

# Cranbrook

When Cranbrook flourished as a centre of the clothing trade, the Flemish weavers laid down three-quarters of a mile of broadcloth when the town was visited by Queen Elizabeth I; another sovereign, Edward I, may have been here in 1299 for the long-legged king, who was nicknamed Longshanks and is best remembered for the crosses he set up after his wife Eleanor died, is reputed to have stayed at the ancient George Hotel. Daniel Defoe knew the neighbourhood of Cranbrook and it is pleasant to think that he may even have written one of the best-loved of all childrens' books here, high up above the Weald amid picturesque wooden houses.

One of the hauntings here is associated with an old house and one with a modern dwelling. The house long known as the Pest House, in Frythe Walk, was built in 1369 and originally used as a hospital or Pestilence House for victims of the plague. Ten years later it became a priest's house but reverted to a hospital in the seventeenth century in order to treat and care for victims of the second plague. Corpses from both outbreaks were buried under the cellars. Later the cellars were re-sealed and the premises altered into two private houses — a Cranbrook gravedigger is said to have occupied one of the cottages, so it might be thought that an aura of death hangs about the place; but this is not so, unless the presence of two or three ghosts can be considered to be morbid.

Robert Neumann, the award-winning Viennese author of thirty-six books, lived at the Pest House for a time and wrote about it — and the ghost — in the book he called *The Plague House Papers* (1958). There he described, as he described to me personally, the apparently well-established ghost of Theresa Benenden, the daughter of an owner of the house in the sixteenth century. Carvings of her initials two inches high are to be seen to this day in the house, one pair over the sitting-room door and another set on a small cupboard door.

Neumann told me that personally his experiences of the haunting had been slight, but convincing. What did interest him was a tape recording which a visitor had produced purporting to be the voice of the ghost girl who had mumbled words that sounded like, 'eight pounds, oh, eight pounds'. This guest had told Robert Neumann that she had clearly seen the ghostly figure of a young woman clad in a night garment, walk out of the room the guest was occupying and disappear into an adjoining room — where other witnesses have reported disturbances. One night a visitor who had no knowledge of any reputed ghost said she saw a woman in her room, wearing a long gown and carrying a candle; many years later a small boy was discovered talking to an invisible lady, early one morning; it was the child who said it was a lady. Neumann called this apartment situated at the top of the house, 'The Ghost Room'.

Interestingly enough Neumann said Theresa never married but she and her father had lived at the Pest House in 1574 and the repetition of the words, 'eight pounds' gained significance as far as Robert Neumann was concerned when he discovered that that was the amount of her annuity. It seems that she was duly paid that amount for five consecutive years and then the payments ceased for some reason; Theresa petitioned for her rights but when she failed to obtain a decision in her favour, she went down into the cellar and committed suicide.

In 1970 a Mrs Irene Newton, baby-sitting for the current occupants, twice claimed that she saw the figure of 'a lovely lady' appear in the inglenook fireplace, emerge into the room, cross the room and disappear half-way up the stairs.

The Deane family lived here in 1975 and before long they were hearing creaks and groans that at first they associated with the old timbers of the house but soon their son William told them that he had seen 'a tall lady' in his bedroom and, on another occasion, he had suddenly come upon a man and a woman standing on the landing and he thought they had tried to stop him walking down the stairs but when he looked back, there was no one there. His description of the 'tall lady' corresponds in some measure with the 'lovely lady' seen by the baby-sitter some six years earlier.

Mrs Newton has stated that her son discovered evidence of a tunnel leading from the inglenook fireplace towards a house called Bakers Cross, several hundred yards away and one writer has suggested that the ghost in the inglenook could be that of a young lady who used to attend illicit assignations by means of the hidden passage. The same writer mentions the fact that Sir John Baker, a savage religious persecutor, was notorious for his womanising and he wonders whether Bakers Cross could once have been associated with Chancellor Baker and that the 'lovely lady' could have been one of his victims, one way or another?

The haunting of a comparatively modern house was reported to me by the then occupant who said everyone in the family had seen the ghost of a boy with fair hair in one of the ground floor bedrooms. They were never able to discover who he was or why he haunted the place but after they all firmly told him to go away whenever they encountered him, he ceased to trouble them!

## Deal

Facing the Goodwin Sands with their cyclic ghost of the *Lady Lovibund,* Deal is full of history and interest and possesses at least one haunted house.

The *Lady Lovibund* is said to have set sail on 13th February 1748 with a large party of guests aboard, celebrating the wedding of the popular captain, Simon Peel. During the night a rival for the favours of his bride, a man named Rivers, deliberately ran the ship aground with all hands lost. This traumatic event and arresting sight is supposed to be re-enacted every fifty years. The ghost ship was reportedly seen on 13th February 1898 and on the same day in 1948; let us hope it will put in an appearance in 1998 when every effort will be made to obtain a scientific record of the event.

I am indebted to Air Commodore R.C. Jonas for this report of a ghostly encounter which was given to him by Betty Cox, the sister of Peter Lucas. The account, as published in May 1949, reads as follows:

'I came to this old smugglers' town this evening to see a friend of mine. He had fixed a room for me at the Manor House, a lovely old Tudor house which is now a country club. I went to my room, changed, and walked out, switching off the light. Then I stopped. I sniffed. Something burning? I put the light on again. Nothing there. "Queer", I thought to myself.

'In the hall I found my host, Peter Lucas, stocky, smiling, sailor-artist. I mentioned the smell of burning. "So you smelt it too", he said. "Lots of people do in that room. It isn't really a smell of burning. It's the smell of candles which have just been snuffed — and it only happens when you put the light out! It is only one of many strange things about this house. Come and look . . . "

'We walked up the ancient oak staircase, and Peter went on: "When I first came to see over the house, I saw an old lady peering at me from an upstairs window. I thought nothing of it. Clearly it must be the housekeeper. But when I'd been over the whole place and had seen nobody about, I asked the previous owner when the old lady would be moving out. He just smiled, 'She'll probably be here for quite a time', he said. 'She's been here since 1800 already . . . it is old Miss Wilkes, who loved the place, and spent the last years of her life scraping the paint off this beautiful period staircase . . . "

'We turned from the staircase at the top — and walked straight into an old-fashioned ship's cabin! "This was the smugglers' cabin of old Admiral Gaunt", explained Peter. "In the Napoleonic Wars he used to smuggle gold to France; and rich cargo to England. He slept in the bunk over there. He would direct a pinpoint of light on a set bearing, and give his fleet of fast smuggling ships the all-clear to cross the Goodwins at half-tide, so that bigger vessels couldn't follow them."

'I struck another match. On one of the tiny window panes I read the name "Lil Gaunt, July 9, 1845". "His wife", explained Peter. "Probably scratched on the glass with a diamond smuggled from Amsterdam."

'As we walked down the stairs, Peter said: "Gaunt died in the room next to yours. At times there is an overwhelming smell of flowers in that room." Peter pushed open the cellar door, and we went down. "There is said to be a hoard of priceless Venetian glass down here", he added. "I've looked but with no luck so far."

'I started scrabbling around the old flagstones, tapping and feeling for loose bricks. "We could do with a bit of Venetian glass at home," I said. But all I found was a lot of dead spiders.'

Dover Castle

## Dover

The high castle at Dover has been used by every race that has ruled in Britain. Here, very probably, there was a British encampment and certainly the Romans were here and the Saxons, and the Normans, and right up to the present day when the muzzles of guns and the curling standard tell us that the old fortress can still guard these shores.

One might think that the 'key of England' would boast a dozen ghosts but spectral visitations seem thin on the ground here and not long ago one of the custodians told me, bluntly: 'We have no ghosts at Dover Castle'. And yet, back in the days of the Napoleonic Wars, when the castle was an important defence against a possible French invasion and two hundred cannon were installed here, there is a story that a young drummer boy, carrying money for the garrison's pay, was ambushed in one of the castle's maze of subterranean passages and there murdered when he would not give up the money. When he was found his head had been completely severed from his body by the unknown ruffians.

On nights of the full moon the ghost of the little drummer boy, headless, is said to walk the battlements; the ghost that everyone has heard about but nobody seems to have seen.

A less alarming ghost once haunted Dover Castle. During the First World War a member of the garrison opened a staircase window to let in, as he thought, his own pet cat, but instead a beautiful white cat hurried past him and disappeared into another room where it vanished without trace. This happened nine mornings in succession and each time the phantom cat, if phantom cat it was, raced through the window and shortly afterwards disappeared. After those nine visits it was never seen again; no one could be found who owned it or knew anything about it but a member of the household died very unexpectedly shortly afterwards and the appearance of the mysterious white cat was regarded as an ill omen.

## Downe

A few years ago Andrew Green told me that Downe Court was haunted. Apparently Brian Thompson, who bought the place in 1962, planned to restore the property to something approaching its former glory and open it to the public but 'four years of effort produced only heart-break, financial loss and despair': the result of an 'overbearing atmosphere of evil', possibly a legacy of the black magic practices carried out there.

According to Andrew Green there are, or were, two specific areas that remained haunted, in spite of two exorcisms being conducted: a bedroom with an adjoining stairway and the former butler's room. An overwhelming feeling of fear is said to have enveloped people at the top of the stairs where a troop of Cavaliers are thought to have hanged a man; while a young lady who slept in the bedroom nearby said she was awakened by a 'thud' and found a ghostly arm, severed at the shoulder, lying on the bed beside her! Other people who have occupied this room have apparently reported 'vague shapes', 'heard the sound of fighting' and seen 'a man dressed like a Cavalier' — but only his head and shoulders!

The ghosts in the former butler's room, says Andrew Green, 'are of a young girl, seen with water dripping down her long dark hair' and another 'mysterious shape' that once stood beside a visitor. It seems a young servant girl was drowned in a nearby lake many years ago and she has been associated with the 'dripping girl'.

Antony Coxe refers to this being the ghost of a girl who was drowned 'in the old moat' and who sobs at a bedside. He also says the ghost of an old man appears here in a barn. Both refer to the photograph taken by Brian Thompson which is said to show seven ghosts — I can't see one that could not be the result of an unusual combination of light and shade!

## Eastchurch, Isle of Sheppey

Here once lived Gabriel Livesey, at Parsonage Farm whose son Michael is depicted on a panel of the family tomb in the church. Also there are a great oak screen, an almsbox cut from solid oak and a pulpit made in the last year of the reign of Elizabeth I and decorated with four tiny heads. Nearby too once stood Sir Thomas Cheney's great sixteenth century house, Shurland.

Michael, when he was a man, sat through every day of one of the greatest trials in history and at the end of it took up his pen and added his name to the death warrant of Charles I.

There must have been many occasions in those far off days when a horse-and-coach clattered along the dusty roadway at dusk and one wonders what traumatic event or climatic condition could have caused one such routine happening to become imprinted upon the atmosphere here, for there have been many reports over the years of such a contraption, trotting silently by the graveyard, usually at dusk. No one knows where it comes from or where it goes to or, for that matter, whom it carries . . .

## Eastry

Many are the tales and stories told about this little place. It is the home of Prior Henry who enriched Canterbury Cathedral with his craftsmanship. There is a tale that a King of Kent murdered the two sons of his sister here and in remorse gave all the land for Minster Church and Minster Abbey. It is almost certain that Thomas Becket hid here from his enemies; a doorway cut out of chalk leads into winding caverns. Here, in the thirteenth century church, where you can see seventeen other churches from the top of the tower, lies one of Nelson's men and here too are some thirteenth century medallions of strange figures, almost faded away; and in the nave a column carved with a mysterious circle that is in fact a method of discovering certain days in the calendar. And here too is the story of a former vicar who so loved his church that shortly before he died, he declared: 'I sware I'll never leave this place . . . '

One day in September 1956, a Surrey bank manager took a photograph of the interior of the church. When the print was developed there was a form of a priest with clasped hands sitting in one of the pews; and we have the assurance that no such person was in the church when the photograph was taken. Some people have felt that the lay-out of the church differs from what it was in 1956. Can the old vicar have kept his word?

# Eastwell near Ashford

A few miles along the Faversham road from Ashford, at a minor junction, there is a large and ornate gateway leading to Eastwell Park. At the other end of the park, on the road near the lake beside the church, an acquaintance told me that some years ago she and four companions suddenly encountered a ghostly two-wheel barouche driven by a man wearing a bow tie who stared straight over the head of his heavily-blinkered horse . . . but I will let Susan Mann tell the story of this strange experience in her own words:

'There were five of us that hot June afternoon and we made our way into an old house down by the lake; the place was empty and boarded-up although the outhouse doors were open. It was all a bit scarey for some reason, and the place had a very strange atmosphere. The house had Gothic-shaped windows on the interior walls dividing the rooms as well as those that looked out of the house. The property was not in bad shape but somehow it felt as though no one had been there for a long time. Outside on the landing stage we saw several dead fish which added to the macabre atmosphere and suggested something old and rotten about that particular spot, for the rest of the lake was abundant in wild life.

'Later, walking back up the lane away from the church, we all heard the sound of horses' hooves. It was hot and sultry and late in the afternoon and we were all feeling rather tired but there was no mistaking the sounds which came nearer and then rounding the bend into the lane ahead of us we saw a horse and trap. As it came nearer we saw it was a kind of two-wheeled barouche of dark oak with a black hood which was folded back. The horse was large and also dark, solid looking and very heavily blinkered, so much so that the leather blinkers covered almost the whole sides of the animal's face and I thought at the time it was difficult to understand how the horse could see anything, certainly we could not see its eyes. I do not know what sort of horse it was but it was quite large and strong looking — and it did not react to us at all.

'Sitting in the barouche was an old man; he sat bolt upright and was staring straight ahead of him with very pale, cold-looking, blue eyes and he had white hair that blew about as he came towards us. He held the reins stiffly in front of him and he was dressed in an old-fashioned black coat and tails with, would you believe it, a yellow polka dot bow tie! The material of his suit was old and looked silky and his top hat was not tall but of medium height. We just stared in amazement, and thought there must be some sort of fancy dress event somewhere — unless the hazy afternoon sun had got the better of us . . . The driver did not seem to see us and was driving past, just staring straight ahead, so I called out, "Evening squire!" but he did not look or move in any way but simply went straight on past us. We all looked at each other and then back along the lane — but there was nothing there! We went backwards and forwards along the lane looking for a place where he might have turned off . . . nothing . . . in any case there had not been time for as soon as he was past we looked round and the horse was not moving very fast . . . that is how we were able to see so much.

Eastwell Park, drawn by George Shepherd c.1830

'So puzzled was I by what we had seen that I did some investigation in Ashford library and discovered that the house had been deserted some fifty years ago. It seems that it could have been the Priests' House for you have to go through the churchyard to get to the house, although on the side facing the Pilgrims Way there are large gates and traces of a track suggesting access for coaches and one of the outhouses would be the right size for a small trap. The house formed part of the estate of Eastwell Park and the main house is large with many bedrooms but was then completely hidden from public view. Study of the local ordnance survey map revealed that there were several other churches in the vicinity but I think the one we saw is called Eastwell, and the lake is now National Trust property. In the library I examined some local records which included an old legend directly associated with this particular house; how every Midsummer Eve reputation has it that "headless horsemen ride from the Pilgrims Way through the house and into the lake"; perhaps this is why the house was deserted!

'A Cambridge friend who is a student of magic and the occult and old legends visited the place with me and said it looked as though the lay of the land was definitely to an old and rigid pattern and the hill behind was probably a "dragon mound". He was very interested in the situation of the church and the house and the lake and thought it likely to have been some kind of ancient place for magic and/or religious practices.

'Some spiritualist friends of mine also looked at the area and found it had a distinct and definitely weird atmosphere. At one time they were interested in buying a haunted house and they made inquiries about this one but were told that it belonged to the church who were not prepared to sell it; no other reason was given.

'On my last visit there were a number of people there, presumably National Trust members, but on our initial visit the place was deserted. The house has been boarded-up again, I noticed. I tried to talk about the house to several local people but they were not very forthcoming. They did say that the church was hit by a bomb during the War, but as far as I could gather no one knew anything about any old gentleman who wore a yellow bow tie and drove a horse and trap . . . at all events I have never had the courage to go there again around Midsummer Eve . . . '

There have been a number of apparently inexplicable incidents reported from this area where the last of the Plantagenets may have lived. The story concerns a 'tiny' cottage by the great house in the park and it is said that here Richard Plantagenet lived.

In 1545 Sir Thomas Moyle was building his great house here and noticed that one labourer was a white-haired man known as Richard. When the rest of the workmen rested or played dice, this man would quietly wander off to some secluded spot and there become absorbed in a book. Not many of the working class could read four-hundred-and-fifty years ago and Sir Thomas was intrigued and eventually won the confidence of the man and heard from him a remarkable story.

Richard said that he had learned to read when he was brought up by a schoolmaster and he knew that from time to time a gentleman came to the house who paid for his food and lodging and schooling and on these occasions he would closely question the boy and ascertain that he was being well-cared for and properly educated.

One day when he was twelve or thirteen this gentleman said he was going to take Richard on a visit. After a long journey on horseback across fifteenth century England they came at last to a vast camp composed of knights and bowmen. The boy was led to an ornate tent where he was greeted by a man wearing a rich suit of armour; a man who put his hands on the boy's shoulders and said, in effect: 'Richard, I am your father, and if I prevail in tomorrow's battle I will provide for you as befits your blood, but if I am defeated, then I shall not see you again . . . ' Puzzled, the boy asked: 'Sir, Father, who are you?' 'I am the King of England today,' replied the man in armour. 'But only heaven knows what I may be tomorrow for the rebels are strong. If the Earl of Richmond wins the day he will seek out all Plantagenets and crush them . . . Tell no one who you are unless I am victorious . . . '

Next day Richard heard the news: the King had lost! The reign of the Plantagenets was over and the Tudors had arrived; it was the end of the long civil wars. Sure enough the hunt was on for anyone related to the dead King and Richard went into hiding and never breathed a word about his royal lineage, passing himself off all through his life as a poor orphan. Yet he had found a certain happiness in honest work and quiet pleasures such as reading.

Sir Thomas Moyle believed the story and he was determined that the last of the Plantagenets should not want in his old age. He had a little house built for Richard in the park and provided for his material needs. So Richard Plantagenet spent his last days hereabouts, walking and reading in the park. He has no place in our history books but he is in the register of burials here and a tomb was long pointed out as his burial place.

Visitors have sometimes reported seeing the shrubs move inexplicably not far from the old jetty, as though someone was walking through them; others have reported on a peculiar atmosphere, chilly and expectant and strangely quiet; still others have reported seeing the figure of a man in strange, mediaeval clothes, walking about the locality, carrying a book . . .

## Five Oak Green

'There is no doubt that this place is haunted,' the landlord of The King's Head told me some years ago. 'I never believed in ghosts until I came here but there's no other explanation . . .'

First there was the movement of small objects in various rooms of the hostelry and this continues to happen from time to time, I understand; but more puzzling still are the sounds of movement from empty rooms, the locking of doors without keys, the 'dark shape' seen moving across the saloon bar, usually around eight o'clock in the evening but sometimes much later, soon after midnight . . .

Especially puzzling were distinct knocks that were heard by the occupants and customers sounding on the back door for which no explanation could ever be found; once, the knocks were heard when the door was under surveillance from both sides! The door to the cellar also seemed to attract the haunting entity and would repeatedly bang inexplicably although it was closed and bolted and bells were heard to ring although they were disconnected and had not worked for years.

Most puzzling of all however was the appearance of an elderly lady, dressed in black, with a white blouse and a large cameo brooch at her throat. This unidentified ghost was seen on at least eight occasions and witnesses include four previous tenants of the haunted King's Head.

## Farningham

An interesting example of reported ghostly happenings achieving credibility through historical occurrences is to be found in the sounds long associated with the Pied Bull Inn here.

Once upon a time one wall of this inn was moved several feet so that the original foundations of the roadway lie within the walls of the present inn; and here, where the wall has been moved outwards, the sound of a coach-and-horses has been heard, apparently passing so close that visitors have hurriedly moved from their comfortable seats in the window . . . the ghost coach-and-horses, it seems, runs where the old road ran.

## Faversham

Burial place of King Stephen, grandson of the Conqueror, this ancient town is full of atmosphere and old houses and seems to slumber with its memories of James II (in the church there is some of his handwriting) and Shakespeare (here as a player in Lord Leicester's company) and one Nicholas Upton, mayor in the year when the Armada came and his scratched initials can be seen to this day.

Among its haunted houses there is the Shipwright's Arms on Hollow Shore where the ghost of a Victorian seaman has been seen: a real old sea-dog with peaked cap, reefer jacket and glaring eyes. Accompanying the apparition there is an overwhelming smell of rum, tobacco and tar, a strange but appropriate aroma. Local gossip has it that after his ship foundered and sank, the old seaman dragged himself across the mud flats towards the welcoming lights of the three-hundred year old weatherboarded inn, but it was all too much for him and he gave a great sigh and died just as he reached the haven of the Shipwright's Arms.

Not too far away from this lonely public house there is a property haunted by the occasional presence of a little girl in Elizabethan costume, a motionless and silent figure that has been seen more than a dozen times in the last few years. No one knows who she is or why she returns for she never speaks (in common with practically all well-authenticated ghosts) or even moves and as soon as she is approached she quickly disappears.

## Folkestone

Houses now stand on the site of an ancient priory and its grounds near the parish church off the Road of Remembrance. They call this area The Bayle and several of the occupants of the cottages abutting the original church wall, where Benedictine monks must once have worked and worshipped, have had curious experiences.

Mrs Ludgate told James Rawlins that on several occasions she has been aware of a group of brown-robed monks seemingly occupied in work that looked like making garden tools. 'They looked quite happy in their work', she said at the time, 'but their clothing was rather ragged'. She wonders whether they could have been mendicants who wear brown habits in contrast to the black robes of the Benedictines.

Other residents who claim to have seen the ghost monks include a married couple who lived here and twice saw a cowled figure on the staircase of their home. This couple also said that they heard the sound of chanting which seemed to come from an area of their front garden, ground that was once part of the priory grounds.

A local postman and a milkman are among other people who do not live at The Bayle and who knew nothing of any reputed ghosts or ghostly happenings until they encountered them. Both said they had heard sounds resembling the 'singing of religious hymns' and had had difficulty in trying to pin-point the exact area that it came from. The postman said in 1977 he saw a 'tall figure wearing a cape or hood, rather like a large duffle coat' glide noiselessly across the road in front of him. He could offer no explanation as to where the figure had appeared from or where it went to and he averred: 'I still don't believe in ghosts!'

The Leas Pavilion Theatre has been reported to have been the scene of odd happenings on occasions. One of the managers had the distinct impression that someone was behind her and indeed is quite certain that she felt someone there but when she turned round the place was deserted — yet the sensation remained: 'Someone I couldn't see was standing there', she said. A set designer, property changers, and other staff at the theatre have experienced similar incidents; trivial in themselves but very puzzling and thought-provoking when viewed collectively. And sufficiently frightening to make all the staff think twice before being alone in the theatre at night.

At one time the disturbances were jocularly put down to 'the old man' and he, whoever he might be, is regarded as being responsible for doors opening and closing by themselves, occasional noises and sounds that have no known physical cause, and the infrequent movement of objects.

## Forest Row

Ashdown House stands in the middle of what is left of Ashdown Forest. It is now a boarding school for boys (Prince Andrew is among former pupils) and special permission was obtained from the headmaster at the time, Mr W.G. Williamson, for a Ghost Club visit some years ago.

Mr Williamson stood on the reputedly haunted stairs and welcomed us to the house, which is a scheduled building, and told us about the somewhat puzzling ghost story.

There has long been talk of the house being haunted by the ghost of Lord Heathfield who died in 1790 and his faltering footsteps are or were reputed to be heard on the main staircase each 6th July, the anniversary of his death; but Mr Williamson reminded us that, as far as we know, Lord Heathfield never even visited the house which in fact belonged to a certain Trayton-Fuller, a Sussex iron-master, who married Lord Heathfield's daughter and the chief historical interest lies perhaps in the fact that the house was built by Benjamin Latrobe who afterwards went to the United States and built part of the Capitol at Washington.

There is nothing, we were told, to suggest that the house is currently haunted but Mr Williamson read out something he had written about the 'supposed spook' many years ago. It is pretty obvious that any ghostly footsteps, if ghostly footsteps there be here each 6th July, are *not* those of Lord Heathfield; unless they are in some way which we do not understand a physical expression of the memory of his daughter. Certainly many books still state that the house 'is haunted by the footsteps of Lord Heathfield'.

## Grafty Green

At the end of May 1982, the attractive ship-board exterior of the King's Head caught my eye and I recalled the tales of strange happenings there over the years.

A famous smuggler known as Dover Bill used to drink at the King's Head; he was a popular member of the local gang of smugglers but, when the Revenue men caught up with him, Dover Bill talked to save his own skin. His former mates were hanged and Dover Bill lost all his popularity and every one of his friends. He died at Grafty Green, the sad shadow of a man with hardly enough to keep soul and body together. After his death there are those who say they felt his presence in the public house, some even say they glimpsed his unmistakable figure in his favourite spot, and many say they sense the feeling of hatred that hung about him like a cloak during his last years . . .

Better known perhaps is the phantom coach-and-horses that has been seen and heard to race past the King's Head on dark and stormy nights, hurtling at breakneck speed towards the church with its linenfold Elizabethan panels, queer images and the grave of one of Queen Elizabeth I's chaplains, Sir Leonelle Sharpe who, we are told, preached fruitfully, lived cheerfully and died joyfully.

It is not easy now to find anyone who admits to seeing the arresting sight of the ghostly coach — some say driven by a headless coachman — but you can still seek out those who have stood at the door of this inn and heard the sound of racing horses, clanking harness and the screams of terrified passengers . . . the psychic echo perhaps of an event of long ago when the four horses pulling the Lenham-bound coach took fright here and bolted. Could they have seen the ghost of Dover Bill?

## Hartley, west of Rochester

In the eighteenth century one Richard Treadwell was landlord at the Fairby House and it is thought to be his ghost, mounted on his favourite iron-grey mare, who makes ghostly visits to Fairby Farm.

A mile or so away Pennis Lane is reputed to be haunted by the ghost of a nun, ravished by one of Cromwell's soldiers, who afterwards hacked off her head rather than let her escape and cause trouble. Andrew Green seems to think the nun was murdered in the 1400s and may be associated with nearby St Johns Jerusalem, a one time establishment of the Knights Hospitallers. At all events years later a skull believed to be that of the murdered nun was unearthed by a farmer and afterwards preserved in the study of Pennis Farm.

## Hawkhurst

The Royal Oak here is a handsome black and white hostelry in the middle of a district that was once a centre for smuggling and famous for its 'Hawkhurst Gang', a notorious group of ruffianly characters who terrorised the area in the middle of the eighteenth century.

Hawkhurst's best remembered resident is probably Sir John Herchel, the third member of the famous Herschel family of astronomers, who studied the stars a century ago. One day two friends who were also astronomers came to Sir John's house, Adams of Cambridge and Leverrier of Paris; they had both discovered Neptune, 2000 million miles away, by arithmetic.

But the ghost at the Royal Oak does not date from either of these long-forgotten days but from a more recent visitor who is reputed to have met his death in Room 22, long known as 'the haunted room'.

A correspondent, Donald West, told me that his researches had shown that at one time a ghostly figure used to walk through the staff quarters of the hotel and disappear into a wall. In May 1984 I spoke to the landlord but he knew nothing of any ghosts for he had only just moved into the mellow inn. A few days later I visited the Royal Oak and he showed me the haunted room and said, not knowing anything about any reputed ghost, he had put his son and a friend in Room 22 for the night and the following morning they had complained that a pair of eyes had seemed to be watching them, first from one side of the window and then from the other; and they also saw a dark figure in the room, moving across the window.

I talked with a barmaid who had been at the Royal Oak for some years; she knew all about the stories of a ghost in Room 22. The ghost was known as 'George' and never appeared anywhere but in that one room. A former licensee claimed to have seen the figure several times and believed that it was the ghost of a man who had died there. I thought that it was interesting that two youngsters had a strange experience in the same room before they knew anything about its ghostly reputation.

## Harrietsham

A mystery man haunts the ancient Ringlestone Tavern here, evidently bent on some mysterious persuit and, perhaps appropriately, mysteriously stopped in the middle of his — or is it her — midnight perambulations.

Could this be the echo of a smuggler, stomping up the cellar steps at dead of night? Of a former landlord, straining an overworked heart? Or a robber, caught in the act? Or a lover, grown careless enough to be found out? Or an unsuspecting husband coming upon his wife and her lover? At all events the sound of footsteps has been heard at this sixteenth century hostelry, times without number, in winter and in summer, in good weather and in foul, on bright nights and on dark ones; always they stamp up the steps from the cellar and at the top they cease. Then follows a sound one might expect if a boot were removed from a foot and thrown to the floor — and then silence.

There is no sound of a second boot being removed; no sound of any subsequent activity; not even any more footsteps, everything else is lost for ever but some incident from the distant past seems to have become partly impressed upon the atmosphere here, to return to puzzle successive occupants and visitors to this lovely old inn.

## Herne

According to Jack Hallam the Fox and Hounds here is, or was, haunted by the ghost of a woman who had been burnt; a phantom form that seemed to be especially visible to young people.

In his *Haunted Inns of England* (1972) Hallam says Alan Reeve-Jones tape-recorded an interview with Philip Bennett in the late spring of 1970, shortly before Bennett went to Australia.

It seems that when he was a lad of twelve and his father was landlord of the Fox and Hounds, Philip was a Boarder at a Catholic school and used to come home most weekends. One night he awoke to find, standing at the foot of his bed, the figure of a grotesque-looking woman; the flesh of her face and hands seeming to be terribly burnt. Philip called out and his brother came into the room and the figure vanished. After that Philip came home at weekends less frequently and when he did he avoided sleeping at the inn as much as he could; nevertheless during the two-and-a-half years that his family were at the Fox and Hounds, he saw the same ghostly figure five times. His mother saw it too and his father but while they tended to dismiss such things, Philip was very frightened.

There were two other ghostly manifestations: a wall of coldness about three feet thick at the top of the landing; and an occasional smell of burnt flowers that often seemed to herald an appearance of the woman who had been burned.

Once, when his father was about to leave the Fox and Hounds, Philip had no option but to spend a couple of weeks at the inn and he used to go to bed with a loaded shotgun on his bed, in case he should be troubled during the night ... One night, after he had smelt the burning flowers and felt the wall of coldness on the landing, he awoke to find the awful figure again standing at the bottom of his bed — he picked up the shotgun and let fly, straight at the head of the figure. The bullets lodged themselves in the wardrobe but of the form he had seen there was now no sign.

Philip's father came in and took the gun away. He was very worried and concerned and so was Philip's mother. He was taken outside and sat in the car with his mother. He could smell the burnt flowers in his bedroom after the figure had disappeared and his mother told him that she had often smelled it too.

Years later, after the War, Philip returned to the Fox and Hounds and asked the landlady whether she knew anything about a ghost in the upstairs room. He then learned that the landlady's son, a boy of nine or ten, had told his mother and father that he had seen the figure of a woman in his bedroom. Their daughter, a girl of nineteen, had never seen the ghost but had encountered the area of coldness and the smell of burning flowers.

In recent years things seem to have become quiescent at the Fox and Hounds and perhaps the ghostly episodes there have now run their course; and yet, who knows, perhaps the frightening apparition of a woman who has been burnt will be seen again when the right person occupies the right room at the right time.

Hever Castle from an old engraving

## Hever

There is little here but a few houses and farms, a church, an inn and the lovely castle. The church, standing at the castle gates, contains an old and worn stone tomb and a brass of 1538 to Thomas Bullen. The effigy shows a man in the rich apparel of a Knight of the Garter, for this is the father of Anne Bullen, the ill-fated second wife of Henry VIII.

Here at Hever there is an oak-panelled chamber that used to be pointed out as the scene of Henry's love-making. Here, in the garden, the king caught his first glimpse of the girl who was to become his unhappy queen. On his return to Westminster, he told Wolsey that he had conversed with a young lady who had the wit of an angel and was worthy of a crown. And here, if we are to believe persistent reports extending over many years, the ghostly figure of Anne glides swiftly over a bridge that spans the River Eden in the castle grounds, especially each Christmas Eve. Canon Pakenham Walsh attended a seance at the castle and believed that contact was made with the ghost of the dead queen.

There is said to be another ghost at Hever; the spectre of a farmer who was robbed and murdered for the gold that he carried but who he was we do not know.

Hever Castle was probably built in the reign of Edward III; in the days of Henry VI it came into the possession of wealthy London merchant Sir Geoffrey Bullen, by whom it was radically transformed and enlarged; after Anne's execution her father, Sir Thomas Bullen, continued to live in disgrace here until his death in 1538 when it was annexed by the King. Two years later he gave it to Anne of Cleves, whom he had just divorced. The glory that was Hever faded then until it was bought by the Astors in 1903 and they restored it to the splendid castle as we know it. But the fascination of Hever is its association with Anne, the mother of Elizabeth I, and it is appropriate that it is her ghost that walks at Hever, albeit at a time when few people are likely to see her.

It is likely that there are secrets and ghost stories yet to come out of Hever. In 1984 a priceless section of a Roman triumphal arch built by the Emperor Claudius, and thought to date from AD51, was discovered. It was acquired by William Waldorf Astor when he was collecting artefacts from the Italian Garden and was still in the garden, unrecognised, when Hever was bought from the Astors in 1983 for a reported £10 million by Yorkshire-based Broadland Properties.

## Higham

Frederick Sanders reports:

'At the edge of Higham marshes, not far from the village of Upper Higham, stand the ruins of a once large and stately mansion, known locally as Great Hermitage. There are several ghost tales and legends associated with this mansion. The first is that of a phantom horseman who, riding a spectral steed, careers down the drive at headlong speed, rides out through the main gateway and gallops off along the road towards the village of Upper Higham. His wrists are chained, so it would appear that he is an escaping captive. This ghost is said to date from the latter half of the eighteenth century.

'The second tale associated with the old place is confined to an upper room where a black woman, presumably a servant, was murdered by a sword thrust. Her blood stained the floorboards and although these boards were repeatedly renewed, the fatal stains returned time and time again. Legend has it that at night a ghostly light lit up this room and could be seen from outside the house shining through the window. People living at the mansion were aware of these ghostly attributes and avoided entering this somewhat gruesome and cheerless chamber whenever possible. This story is said to date from about 1800-1820.

'In the old days Great Hermitage was also said to be haunted by the figure of a smiling lady who was seen by many people, residents, local people and visitors. She would quietly ascend the main staircase and then slowly turn before entering a room on the landing or passage-way above and anyone who happened to be in the room at the time would see her disappear through a wall in the room.

'In the hall, an artist, now dead for well over a hundred years, painted a fresco that took him many long weeks of toil. His laborious task completed, he placed a curse upon the fresco: anyone who at any time should deface or destroy the work, would be cursed with a thousand ailments. This happened early in the nineteenth century and the event became known as "The Curse of a Thousand Curses". It was said that the eventual disappearance of the mansion itself was a direct result of this curse.

'Villagers of Higham, before the First World War, would tell of the ghostly sound of a horn that was sometimes heard echoing across the desolate marsh-lands late at night. Coinciding with the sounding of the horn, other villagers reported seeing the figure of a black-cloaked and cowled monk stalking across the grounds before disappearing into the empty mansion, by way of the under-croft.

'The ghost of this Black Monk is said to be linked with the location of a hidden treasure chest and with a secret tunnel, a mile or more long, that reputedly runs under the Higham marshes to the River Thames in the distance. The treasure is supposed to be hidden in the vicinity of the old undercroft. The ghostly Black Monk is said to date from the latter half of the eighteenth century.

'The fragmentary ruins of Great Hermitage are to be found down a lane off the village road of Higham, near the edge of the desolate Higham marshlands that stretch away to the grey waters of the Thames in the distance. The mansion was erected during the eighteenth century by Sir Thomas (? Richard) Head and served as a home for several well-known county families. Its once beautiful lawns, flower-beds and terraced walks are all gone but a few tall deciduous trees and evergreens surround the outlying park. There is also a lovely rhododendron walk consisting of these flowering shrubs in various colours. Some years ago a row of peculiarly deformed and twisted trees lined the top of the wall of the upper terrace: they had a very ghostly appearance, especially in silhouette on a light night. After the departure of the last of the old families from Great Hermitage, it was taken over by a brotherhood of monks. When the monks left the mansion, about 1912, they disinterred the remains of one of their brethren who had died there, and had been buried in the lower garden beneath the trees, and took the remains to their new abode.

'During the 1914-1918 War the mansion was converted into a V.A.D. hospital and then for over twenty years it remained empty and neglected and built up a great reputation for itself as a haunted building. In the late 1930s the old place caught fire and was burned down to a crumbling ruin.'

During a night-time vigil at the ruins in November 1940 Frederick Sanders thought at first that he glimpsed the ghostly Black Monk. His report reads:

'Shortly after my arrival I was walking across the upper ruins and then, by sheer instinct, I stopped short and found myself upon the very brink of a drop which would have precipitated me into the old cellars with possibly a broken arm or leg as a reward. I made a good search of the terraces and their steps and also the wooded lower grounds.

'As I stood on top of the upper terrace and gazed at the ruined mansion, I heard the sounds of footsteps as if someone was walking through the dried undergrowth and brush beneath the tall trees in the lower gardens. For about a minute these sounds continued and then stopped as abruptly as they had begun.

'I now walked along the top of the flight of stone steps leading from the back lawn down to the first terrace of the gardens; the top of this terrace has a wall lined with the weirdly twisted trees . . .

'Looking down the steep flight of steps and across the walk or path of the terrace I saw what appeared to be a shadow; nothing clear-cut or defined, but rather vague and hazy: a shadow resembling the shape of a man, and a man attired in a cowl and a long cloak. This seemed almost too good to be true! Was it eye-strain brought on by night conditions? An hallucination, caused by strain, and the wish to see the cowled form of the Black Monk of Higham?

'I went down the steps and the "shadow" appeared to retreat before me (it was not fully detached, but merged with the foliage adjacent to the side of the stone steps). When I had almost reached the bottom it disappeared – or merged into the foliage. I walked up the steps again, reached the top, turned around and gazed down. The "shadow" was still below. Again I stepped down and the "form" moved away and when near the base merged into the greenway as before. Again I ascended: once more looked down; still the "shadow" persisted! I descended a third time and the same thing happened.

'It was not eye-strain; neither was it an hallucination. It was some high foliage, part of a larger mass, which had the form of a man and in the poor light of the stars, appeared shadowy and, as I slowly descended the steps each time it "moved" as I gradually out-phased it and the "shadow" disappeared as it became part of the larger or parent mass of evergreen.'

## Hollingbourne

Little appears to be known about a much-altered house here, Eythorne Manor, but it may date from about 1400 when it could have been the hall house of a yeoman, for it is a typical Wealden building with a large hall and central fireplace.

A former occupant of one of the three cottages that comprised Eythorne Manor thirty years ago maintained that she and her two children experienced 'ghostly phenomena' there for some ten years.

Times without number the children, a boy and a girl, said they were frightened by 'something walking on the stairs' and although their mother too heard the heavy tread of 'something' invisible going up the stairs on many occasions, she tried to persuade the children that the sounds that worried them must surely be due to the wind, or the creaking of old wood, or even rodents: anything would be preferable to ghosts! Not that she ever really convinced the children any more than she was herself convinced that the strange sounds had a rational explanation.

In an adjoining cottage, when she was no more than four years old, little Sally Brunger occupied a room at the back of the house. One evening, as she prepared for bed, she surprised her mother by saying she wondered whether she would see the 'little old lady' that night. Careful and guarded questioning elicited the fact that a 'lady in grey' sometimes came to visit the little girl in bed and the old woman would relate stories to the child but, Sally complained, the 'lady in grey' spoke in such a low voice that she could hardly hear what she said.

After this Sally's mother would creep quietly past her daughter's open bedroom door and sometimes she would hear the child talking quietly to someone. According to Sally, the little old lady in grey who stood at the foot of her bed when she did not sit on it, liked to be talked to. When the family eventually left the house Sally was quite upset at the thought that she would not see her nocturnal visitor again.

Sally's mother never saw the figure but she did hear, several times, a strange slithering sound, almost like someone passing by dressed in a long dress of silk or taffeta, and she also heard this sound in her daughter's room when it was completely deserted as far as anything visible was concerned; she also noticed a 'clammy, cold feeling' at the spot in the bedroom where Sally told her the 'lady in grey' always stood.

Once a short man in an old-fashioned black suit was seen in the corner of the garden, seemingly watching the house. He made no response when he was spoken to and a moment later he had completely disappeared. There seemed no possible explanation as to where he could have gone and the mystery was never solved but the then occupants learned that a similar figure and various puzzling incidents had been reported by neighbours and visitors and it came to be accepted that Eythorne Manor was indeed haunted — especially when a gentleman living at the other end of the property said he had seen the figure of a lady in grey that he could not account for; a figure that moved silently along a corridor towards that part of the property where the same figure had been reported!

In the seventies the Simmons family, who had bought the place twenty years earlier, said they had always been aware of an unseen presence in the house and of a cold and rather weird feeling in several parts of the property. At the window of one of the front bedrooms a man's face was repeatedly seen at one time; and there was an isolated and completely inexplicable appearance of a little man wearing a green suit in a room on the ground floor.

Mrs Sheila Simmons told Andrew Green that soon after they moved into the house she heard the slithering noise in the 'haunted bedroom'. 'It was not at all nice', she said. 'Standing in the empty room you suddenly heard this sound, just like silk being dragged across the floor towards you . . . once it frightened me so much that I ran out of the house . . . '

Several times Mrs Simmons heard the sound of a lot of people talking when she was alone in her sitting room; the sound seemed to come from next door but at the time the building next door was empty; or at least empty as far as human occupants were concerned.

Over the years various odd things have happened at Eythorne Manor. Objects have moved by themselves; sounds like clinking coins have been heard; a transparent dog was seen to walk through a closed door; knocks have been heard for which no normal explanation was ever discovered; footsteps have been heard running round the outside of the house . . .

In May 1984, Mrs Sheila Simmons told me that nothing of any real significance had happened for some years. It was all very 'lively' when her daughters were teenagers and the house was being altered and restored. Now the girls are married and away and the restoration work was completed years ago. 'However', went on Mrs Simmons, 'some days I feel like a usurper in my own house. My youngest daughter stayed with her family over Christmas 1983, and in the 'solar' bedroom (where they slept) they all felt as though they were being watched.'

Speculation as to the origin of the mysterious happenings at Eythorne Manor over the years have been ingenious and intriguing but it is merely speculation since sadly so little is known of the history of this interesting house.

Here at Hollingbourne once stood the old house, Greenway Court, one-time home of the influential and romantic Colpepper family. Later the Elizabethan manor house with its three stacks of Tudor chimneys became a farmhouse and, although there are many local stories of the Colpepper family who lived here from 1684 to 1758, most of them are probably apocryphal, and it is the ghostly presence of a less well-known lady that has been seen in the vicinity of the fifteenth century church.

Lady Grace Gethin died when she was only twenty-one and this seventeenth century young lady is buried here but she has a monument in Westminster Abbey, where she is shown kneeling and holding the book which has caused her name to be remembered, albeit by means of an accident.

After her death her executors published as her work a bundle of papers that she had left and it was then discovered that the manuscript was, to a great degree, extracts from other peoples' works. However the book enjoyed considerable success before the truth was discovered and while it can be regarded as a literary imposture, it does seem that the whole affair was perfectly innocent. Perhaps her ghost walks until her name is completely cleared or perhaps the remarkable experience she had the day before she died has left behind conditions condusive to the reappearance of this remarkable young lady.

The memorial stone in the church tells the story: 'Having the day before her death most devoutly received ye Holy Communion (wch she said she would not have omitted for ten thousand worlds) she was vouchsafed in a miraculous manner an immediate prospect of her future blisse for ye space of two houres to ye astonishment of all about her and being (like St Paul) in an inexpressible transport of joy (thereby fully evidencing her foresight of the heavenly glory) in inconceivable raptures triumphing over death and continuing sensible to ye last she resigned her pious soul to God and victoriously entered into rest.' Be that as it may previous rectors, churchwardens and members of the congregation have said they have glimpsed the ghostly form of Lady Grace, gliding quietly along the church path or kneeling beside the tomb where her bones have rested for two hundred years.

Another ghost here is the well-known but unlamented Wild Rider: a man on horseback who rides at breakneck speed on a stretch of the old Pilgrims' Way near Hollingbourne where the road runs north of the A20 towards Charing.

There have been many reports of the arresting spectral appearance being seen in daylight, the seemingly foolhardy rider, pressing his steed ever faster while the creature races along, its nostrils flaring; but oddly no sound accompanies the fast-fleeing horse and rider.

On the other hand at night the same area is haunted by the *sounds* of a horse and rider, galloping at full speed along the ancient roadway, but at night there are no reports of anything being *seen*.

Another horse-and-rider ghost haunts the same stretch of the Pilgrims' Way and looks and sounds perfectly normal, except that the rider wears a wide-brimmed hat and very ornate spurs. This is thought to be the ghost of a man named Duppa who lived at nearby Hollingbourne House and was famous for his riding exploits. Eventually he and his horse were killed when he attempted to jump the high wrought-iron gates leading to his house. But as ghosts he and his steed are quiet and well-behaved, sometimes riding quietly alongside a visiting rider and even, it has been said, politely greeting them before suddenly and inexplicably disappearing without trace leaving the traveller puzzled, bemused and bewildered.

## Hook Green near Lamberhurst

A few miles north, off the 2169, you come to beautiful Bayham Abbey, founded in 1200. These spectacular ruins are said to be haunted by spectral monks, phantom bells and ghostly voices. They are perhaps the most beautiful ruins in all England and are under government control.

Richard Church found Bayham a place of absolute peace as well it might be for it once housed a community of Premonstratensian Canons, a strict Order, a reformed sect of the Augustinians. The English branches of the Order were

Bayham Abbey in the eighteenth century

called White Canons, from their thick woollen cloaks of undyed material, and it must have been a picturesque sight to see such figures about the abbey in those medieval days, so isolated and silent even today.

Special arrangements were made for a Ghost Club visit to Bayham some years ago and everyone was impressed by what must have been a wonderful building; some idea of the grandeur can be obtained from what remains, especially the view from the choir looking towards the nave and west entrance. Part of a holy-water stoup is among the remains of Bayham Abbey and, in a niche, the forlorn remains of a tomb. Nearby one of the members reported an overwhelming impression of the presence of a holy person, a monk or an abbot. After a few seconds the impression completely disappeared.

Ghost stories connected with Bayham concern spectral monks, white-clad and tonsured, winding in procession noiselessly amongst the ruins at midnight on moonlit nights; the smell of burning incense (not used here for nearly five hundred years) has been reported by visitors; and also sweet music; the sound of revelry; voices chanting in unison and a faint but distinct impression of distant bells.

The road from Hook Green to Bell's Yew Green is reputedly haunted by a phantom car which disconcertingly disappears when approaching vehicles are about a hundred yards away.

# Lamberhurst

Harry Price says in his monumental *Poltergeist Over England* (1945): 'An unusual case was reported in the *Daily Mail* dated 28th May 1906. At Furnace Mill, Lamberhurst, lived Mr J.C. Playfair (sic). One morning during this month of May he went to his stables and found all the horses had been turned the reverse way round in their stalls. Their tails were in the mangers and their heads were where their tails should have been. One of the horses was missing. Mr Playfair hunted high and low and, happening to look into the hay-room, nearby, discovered the horse. How it got there is still a mystery, because *a partition had to be knocked down to get it out.* The doorway of the hay-room was barely wide enough for a man to enter. Other phenomena included the removal of some heavy barrels of lime which were hurled down the wooden stairs; a large waterbut, "too heavy for any human being to move", was overthrown; and locked and bolted doors were found open. No one could approach the mill unseen, and two watch-dogs were on guard. There was no young girl in the case but we read of a "young son".'

Some years ago I took a party of Ghost Club members to Kent and we sought out the site of the allegedly haunted mill, in its day one of the most important and successful of the Kent iron furnaces; and it was not until I read the March 1983 number of *Bygone Kent* that I learned the mundane solution of this particular 'poltergeist'. The article in question is entitled 'Gloucester Furnace and the Haunted Mill, Lamberhurst' by Adrian Harland and I acknowledge his kind permission to reproduce here the latter part of his article:

'During the early years of this century Furnace Mill became a notorious place for ghost hunting. The then owner, Mr Tom Playfoot, had reported certain unaccountable happenings and manifestations in the old mill house and about the farm. The word spread quickly throughout the village and surrounding countryside until the local inhabitants were quite convinced they were sheltering one of the most enterprising, audacious and mysterious "ghosts" ever to be recorded. Local newspaper reporters flocked to the "haunted mill" at Lamberhurst and very soon the National Press were taking a keen interest in the strange experiences encountered in this Wealden village.

'The *Daily Mail* sent a reporter to investigate, but he found Mr Playfoot was rather reluctant to discuss the matter, for hundreds of unwanted people from the towns and villages for miles around had invaded his farm in search of the "ghost" and the last thing he desired was further publicity.

'Despite various efforts taken by Mr Playfoot to thwart the "ghost", locked and bolted doors swung open, his horses were changed from stable to stable and frequently turned round in their stalls so that their backs were against the mangers, hay was cut and scattered about the hayloft, while in the toolhouse barrels of lime weighing hundredweights were flung down the stairs. These and many other strange things were reported to happen in rooms that were locked, barred and bolted while people watched and listened outside, but nothing was ever seen.

'One morning, according to Mr Playfoot, as he was working near one of the stables the lock was screwed off the stable door. He substituted a bolt only to find shortly afterwards, much to his utter amazement, the bolt had been removed and the lock neatly restored to its place. Hoards of people came to view Furnace Mill and scores of postcards of the "Haunted Mill" were sold at the village post office.

'The local police attempted to investigate the circumstances, but without success. They were just as mystified as Mr Playfoot at the strange happenings. Meanwhile, the *Daily Mail* reported "something like alarm exists among the scattered inhabitants of Lamberhurst, Horsmonden and Goudhurst, and they hope that the 'ghost' as they firmly believe it to be, will confine its operations to Furnace Mill".

'Country people are by nature superstitious and stories of the "ghost" at Furnace Mill still persist among some of the older generation. While the Mill is an eminently appropriate home for a "ghost", being quietly situated in a wooded hollow a quarter of a mile from the main road and steeped in history, the time has come to lay this particular "ghost" once and for all. All the weird happenings reported by Mr Playfoot were quite true, but his property was "haunted" by none other than his young son Tom. The lad had taken to reading ghost stories and thought Lamberhurst a trifle dull and devoid of phantoms. He took it upon himself to remedy the situation by inventing a ghost, but his prank was so successful it went much further than he had ever intended. We can only speculate as to what his father said to him when he finally found out!'

The great house here is nearby moated Scotney Castle. Fragments from the fourteenth century remain, primarily the Ashburnham Tower, emplacements of three other towers and the four angle piers of the gate-house which still flank the entrance. The 'new house' (where Prime Minister Margaret Thatcher has a flat) was built between 1837 and 1842 and is now the home of Mrs Elizabeth Hussey, the widow of Christopher Hussey, the architectural historian whose family was associated with Scotney for over two hundred years. The present house overlooks a deep valley with the ruined mediaeval castle in its moat lying directly below; many people who should know regard Scotney as one of the most beautiful gardens in England.

The fourteenth century circular tower, roofed in a witch's hat of tiles, has a singular ghost: 'the figure of a murdered man, dripping with water, who hammers at the great door of Scotney, seeking retribution'. The story is said to date from the eighteenth century when some members of the Darell family, who lived at Scotney for over three-hundred-and-fifty years, took to smuggling and when hard pressed by Revenue men, engaged in a lengthy skirmish and one of the Revenue officers was killed and his body thrown into the moat . . . it is supposed to be the ghost of this man, wet with ghostly water, that has been seen and heard on occasions, crawling up out of the moat and banging on the old door . . .

When I was there some years ago with a party of Ghost Club members Mrs Hussey (who lived with her husband near to my home in Hampshire all through

Scotney Castle in 1783

the last War) was kind enough to show us the interior of the old castle which is not open to the general public. There, under the stairs, we examined a famous hiding-place leading to a small room under the roof, from which a low door opens into another room which has a way out to the stairs above and down a chimney place to ground level. The flooring of the first room is raised above the level of the landing so that anyone seeking secret apartments would suspect the existence of a second secret room but, even if all three rooms were found, it is likely that anyone hiding there would escape for part of the floor under the door between the two little rooms slides back, revealing a sloping shaft down which a man could squeeze into a tiny stone chamber.

It was in this small apartment that a Roman Catholic priest, Father Richard Blount, and his servant, Bray, remained in hiding for a week while the Darells and their servants were sent to Newgate Gaol and their enemies thought they thoroughly searched the whole premises. In the end Blount's servant, Bray, gave himself up and the searchers departed. In fact for seven years from 1591 Scotney was the secret abode and centre for the missionary activities of this celebrated Jesuit. He had an even more spectacular escape at Christmas 1598 when he and Bray hid in 'a secret place digged in a thick stone wall' and the search went on for ten days. Towards the end of that period Mrs Darell, released from the gatehouse where she had been confined with her children, noticed the end of a girdle protruding from the secret entrance to the hiding place and she succeeded in warning Blount to pull it in — but she was overheard. The searchers renewed their efforts and after examination and testing they began to batter down the adjacent masonry and would surely have found the priest in his hiding

Scotney Old Castle and moat

place had not heavy rain forced them to postpone operations for the time being. In the circumstances Blount resolved to make a dash for freedom that night and Bray boldly entered the Great Hall where the men were having supper and raised a false alarm, saying thieves were stealing the horses from the stables ... everyone hurried over the bridge while Blount, clambering over a wall, plunged into the icy moat and swam across. On the other side he was joined by Bray, who had escaped in the darkness and confusion caused by his story, and the pair made good their escape, probably to Twissenden, in Kilndown, where elaborate hiding places existed ... could it be his dripping form that clambers up out of the moat?

Mysteries abound at Scotney. The Darell owner in 1720, Arthur Darell, died abroad and his body was brought home for burial. As the body was being lowered into the grave, a tall figure in a black cloak, whom nobody recognised, was heard to say: 'That is me they think they are burying ...' before hurriedly leaving the scene and, apparently, he was not seen again. More than a century later the then sexton, John Bailey, came upon a massive iron-studded coffin during the course of preparing for a burial, and on raising the lid discovered that the coffin contained only heavy stones.

Some historians have suggested that Arthur Darell was the smuggler who killed a Revenue man and, to overcome the problem of being outlawed, he faked his own funeral; others assert that family quarrels and ill-feeling could have been the motive for his 'disgrace'.

Five hundred years earlier, in 1259, one Walter de Scoteni, whose family gave the castle its name, is said to have been induced by William de Valence to administer poison to the Earl of Gloucester and other nobles at a feast at the Bishop of Winchester's palace. The Earl's brother and some other nobles died but the Earl himself escaped death narrowly, it is said, with the loss of his nails, teeth and skin. Walter de Scoteni, who had been steward to Gilbert de Clare, Earl of Gloucester, is said to have been hanged on suspicion of having poisoned the Earl and his brother William de Clare and his estates were forfeited and reverted to the Crown. At all events the de Scotenis disappear at this stage from the history of Scotney. Could it be the ghost of this early member of the Scotney family who has reportedly returned on rare occasions to manifest his presence by footsteps and the sound of whispering?

As the excellent guide by Christopher Hussey says, there are times when the combinations of shape, colour and texture make the castle seem 'the insubstantial fabric of a dream' and it must seem likely that the chequered history of Scotney has left behind some remnants of its varied occupants and vivid episodes of the bright tapestry that is the history of Scotney, one of the most impressive places in all England.

## Leeds

The famous moated castle, once among the most impregnable strongholds in England, has seen many owners and has been used for many purposes. Here Richard II was imprisoned and the Irish chieftain Desmond, and here the fifteenth century Duchess of Gloucester was tried as a witch.

Founded by the Saxons, continued by the Normans, extended by the Plantagenets and the Tudors, still half of what we see today was built as recently as 1822. Among the grim stories that are part of the history of Leeds Castle is the discovery, just over a century ago, within these massive walls, of the skeleton of a man with, behind him, the remains of food and water. Here one can see the little pink shoes once worn by Anne Bullen, Henry VIII's second wife, and here too one can look at a secret drawer where five hundred golden coins were found, thought to have been hidden there by Elizabeth I.

It is a fairy tale place and it has a sort of family ghost and a phantom black hound. The fearsome dog is thought to date from the fifteenth century when Henry VI's aunt was found guilty of practising 'necromancy, witchcraft, heresy and treason' and spent the rest of her life imprisoned here. At all events the rare appearances of this phantom animal have seemed to herald bad luck for the castle owners and so the 'Black Dog of Leeds' is considered a harbinger of ill-omen.

The owners of Leeds Castle before the First World War, the Wykeham-Martins, used to tell stories of the unexplained appearance and disappearance of a medium-

Leeds Castle from an old engraving

sized, curly-haired, retriever-type dog that would suddenly appear in a room and then as suddenly disappear. Sometimes the ghost dog would seem to disappear into a wall or fade into a closed door and although it was generally regarded as a harmless phantom there were those in the family who associated appearances of the 'animal' with death, disaster, bad-luck and ill-health.

And yet appearances of the ghost dog of Leeds did not always, apparently, portend doom and disaster and Jimmy Wentworth Day related to me a story he had first heard from a member of the Wykeham-Martin family.

One quiet autumn evening this lady was sitting at one of the great mullioned bay-windows and as she looked out across the moat to the five hundred acre park beyond, watching the setting sun, a ghost dog suddenly appeared in the room. No sound accompanied the appearance but something told her to look round and when she did so she saw a large black dog walking across the room. She had no feeling of apprehension or sensation of coldness or any awareness of anything unusual happening and she looked at the dog in mild wonder, thinking the door must have been ajar to allow his entrance and, since she did not recognise the animal, she thought he must be a new addition to the household.

As she prepared to make friends with the animal, which appeared to be a perfectly solid and normal creature, it completely ignored her, approached the wall opposite the window and simply vanished into the wall! Very surprised at this turn of events, the lady left her seat by the window and prepared to cross the room and examine the wall at the place where she had seen the dog disappear.

Even as she left the window-seat and before she reached the wall she was heading for, the whole of the bay-window, including the window seat she had just been occupying, cracked, broke away from the wall and crashed into the moat below! Had she not seen the dog, she pointed out to Jimmy Wentworth Day, she would most certainly have plunged to her death that day with a ton of centuries-old bricks and masonry on top of her.

## Leigh, near Tonbridge

This is a beautiful village with an Elizabethan house, Hall Place, and a thirteenth century church with a fascinating brass to an unknown lady who died in 1580, showing a woman kneeling and an angel blowing a trumpet beside an open coffin, on which is inscribed the words: 'Farewell a l ye until ye come to me'. Neither have ghosts, as far as I know, but the property known as Ramhurst, a manor and later a farm, was long reported to boast a headless woman dressed in a grey robe who walked about the estate.

When Ramhurst was a manor house it was owned by the influential Colpepper family. In 1857 it passed into the hands of a retired Indian Army officer. He and his wife were repeatedly disturbed by mysterious voices, phantom footsteps, the sound of rustling silk and other sounds of someone being present, but there was never any explanation for the strange noises.

Once the brother of the mistress of the house and the cook both heard the mysterious voices at the same time. Thinking it must be his sister calling for help, although it was the middle of the night, the startled man hurriedly grabbed a gun and rushed upstairs, only to find his sister sleeping peacefully. At the bedroom door he met the cook who had also heard voices and had come to see whether she could help her mistress: they both looked at her and then at each other. Whose voices had they heard: there was no one else in the house at the time?

During the course of a visit by a friend who professed to have mediumistic powers, things seemed to become more definite and distinct. On her arrival this friend stated that she distinctly saw the ghosts of an elderly couple standing at the front door watching her arrival and subsequently the same ghostly couple were seen by the owner of the house and by his wife on several occasions; once she walked right through the apparitions!

The visitor claimed to make contact with the ghosts who said their surname was Children. Dame Children, who appeared to wear silk brocade and a lace collar, was always the most distinct figure but she said she was accompanied by her husband, Richard. They said they had once lived at Ramhurst and they loved and cherished the place so much that they could not bear to leave it, even after the death of their physical bodies. They added that they intended to haunt the place until it was again in the possession of the Children family.

Historical researchers claim to have discovered that a man named Simon Children lived at nearby Hildenborough in 1379 and that one of his descendants married one Ann Saxby. It was a family named Saxby who bought the house from the Colpeppers and a descendant of Ann Children was named Richard; he died at Ramhurst in 1753. Notwithstanding the assertions of the ghostly pair there do not appear to have been any psychic disturbances at Ramhurst for many years now.

The Shallows are a small expanse of fast running shallow water that make up part of the River Medway between Tonbridge and the village of Leigh. Kevin Griffin tells me there have been several interesting ghost sightings here, all centred around the main railway line that runs past the Shallows; and the sightings have all been reported by fishermen.

In the summer of 1976 a group of men were fishing at night near the railway line when, just after midnight, they all saw the figure of a young lady dressed in red standing on the railway embankment, seemingly calling for help. They hurried to her aid and saw her run up the embankment opposite, and on to the railway line — and there she disappeared. Investigation into the matter by Kevin and Sean Griffin revealed the fact that, many years ago, a nineteen year old girl had committed suicide by throwing herself under a train at this spot.

In the same area in the late 1800s a goods train ploughed off the tracks and into a gravel pit adjacent to the railway line. Both the men forming the train crew were reported drowned and from time to time the ghost of one of them has been seen walking along the railway line at night, swinging his lantern. Most of the sightings of this ghost have been reported by fishermen as they walked home at night along the railway line on summer nights.

On the opposite side to the gravel pit, with the railway running between the two, there is an area of marshland. Here, on warm summer nights, balls of marsh gas are sometimes released from the ground and float and bob about in the warm currents of air above the railway line and when conditions are right they ignite and burst into flame causing the so-called Will-o'-the-Wisp and Kevin Griffin wonders whether this physical phenomenon could be the explanation for the fishermens' swinging lantern ghost?

## Lydd

In common with many of Kent's old inns, the century-and-a-half old George Hotel in the High Street here was once used by smugglers and there used to be a secret passage leading to the nearby church where contraband may have been hidden in some of the tombs which show traces of once having had sliding panels fitted to them. Occupants of the hotel, and also visitors who have no knowledge of the likely history of the George, have reported curious incidents that suggest connotations with smuggling.

Sounds, muffled and stealthy, in the middle of the night; the nocturnal footfall that has no material explanation; unseen forms that cause the flooring to vibrate; doors opening and closing, violently, of their own accord; even the occasional phantom form: all have been reported here over the years by different people on different occasions. No doubt some of the sounds have a natural explanation, old floorboards shrinking and swelling and unexpected gusts of wind perhaps; but there do seem to have been rather a lot of similar experiences in particular parts of the George Hotel.

## Lympne

Lympne Castle has been a Roman watch-tower and fortress, an Anglo-Saxon outpost, a stockaded camp, a Norman castle, a home of the archdeacons of Canterbury (including Thomas Becket), a Tudor fortified residence, a farm, the haunt of smugglers and a look-out post during the Second World War. Some of these diverse uses and different periods, if not all of them, have left behind ghostly forms and paranormal happenings.

In Roman times, when the watch-tower was one of five which the Romans, under Theodosius the Younger, built along the southern coast of Britain to watch for the approach of Saxon pirates, legend and folk memory has it that a soldier of Rome, on watch duty in the east tower, accidentally fell to his death and ever since, all through the succeeding years, unexplained footsteps have been heard mounting the tower steps . . . but no footsteps are ever heard coming down the stairway.

Ancient documents and local folklore tell of six Saxons fleeing from the Normans and it seems that this terrifying ordeal has become imprinted on the atmosphere here for a ghostly group of six Saxons have been seen inside the Castle. The story goes that the Normans discovered the Saxons in their hiding place and promptly slaughtered them; and it is interesting that these ghostly figures, shadowy and silent, bring with their sudden and unexpected appearance, a sense of despair and doom.

A previous tenant of Lympne Castle, Mrs Henry Beecham, sister-in-law of Sir Thomas Beecham, reported seeing yet another ghost, a form in Tudor costume; while various sounds and vague forms that have been heard and seen here over the years are thought to date from the period when smugglers used the place. Until a few years ago, in the glebe meadow, at the back of the church, there stood a little wooden shanty that the smugglers used as a look-out. From this little building a wide view could be obtained of the marshes stretching down to the sea and, while cargoes were being unloaded, a keen look-out could be kept and the approach of any officers could be signalled to the smugglers on the beach below.

Lympne Castle in the eighteenth century

Nearly twenty years ago now I took a party of Ghost Club members to Lympne Castle and Mr and Mrs Harry Margary told us they had heard mysterious footsteps and other noises which they were totally unable to account for.

One of our members, over here on a visit from South Africa, sent me a note of her experiences during this visit: 'The guide mentioned a room where monks had lived and that intrigued me... when I entered the room I stretched out my hands as I would if I were dowsing... at first nothing happened but as I moved around the room I began to get vibrations and my breath came in gasps; I found that my head was beating furiously and my whole body seemed to be twisted ... I approached another member, Eric Maple, saying I thought something terrible had happened in the room and then, in the presence of several of the members, I repeated the experiment and the result was exactly as before. The effect on me was one of devastation and exhaustion...'

I asked Eric Maple to let me have an independent note of the incident and also to put on record yet another ghost story he had heard at Lympne and this he was good enough to do: 'Following the lecture on the Castle's history, given by our hostess, I decided to enquire whether there had been any ghostly manifestations in recent times. From what we had been told most of the hauntings appeared to be in the nature of folklore or hearsay, including the legend of the Roman centurion who once walked the castle stairs.

'It seemed highly improbable that there had been absolutely nothing of this character within the experience of those now living . . . and with this in mind I asked one of the ladies employed at the Castle if she knew of any such occurrences. She replied that while she had no personal experience of this type of phenomena the two kitchen girls were supposed to have heard the mysterious cry of a baby from an empty room in one of the towers earlier in the year. The two girls, whose names I had no time to record, told me the following remarkable story.

'On Whit Monday 1967, whilst working in a room in one of the towers they had heard, on separate occasions, the crying and whimpering of a baby in the room beneath them. Alarmed they had hurried down but had found the room empty. They were absolutely astounded to discover that no baby was in the Castle at the time.

'I was intrigued by this story which had something in common with the tradition I had investigated at Reculver last year in which the sound of a crying child had been heard on a site where, it had afterwards transpired, a child had been sacrificed by the Romans.

'I had just obtained a description of the room, finding that it was situated on the floor above that where the Club had just lunched, when one of the Club members, a lady, rushed into the kitchen begging me to accompany her to one of the towers where, according to her, "something horrible had once taken place". I followed her and found myself in the very room where the crying was supposed to have been heard. Here I discovered her together with several others including my wife Dora and Beata Bishop.

'The lady who had reported the matter to me was almost hysterical, walking up and down and indicating with her hand the place on the floor where she felt sure some terrible thing had occurred. The onlookers looked extremely embarrassed, I must say. She did this several times, describing with outstretched hand the precise area which had given off the macabre sensation. When she had recovered a little I asked if her impressions included any idea of the nature of the tragedy, but she was quite unable to help further.

'It transpired that she was a dowser but she was without her pendulum that day and appeared to be using her hands instead. After she left the room I told the others the story of the crying baby and suggested that this might possibly indicate a further example of a 'foundation sacrifice' haunting. We left shortly afterwards and I was unable to pursue the matter further but, as you know, I. reported it to you within a matter of minutes.'

## Maidstone

Frederick Sanders was fascinated by the strange atmosphere he encountered in the Baxter Print Room at Maidstone Museum. He told me: 'The museum at Maidstone is a fine, large building, well-lighted, clean and in no way depressive as buildings of a like nature sometimes tend to be. It has a vast number of rooms of all sizes, many stairways and corridors and passages. It is situated not far from the River Medway and is surrounded on three sides by the beautiful public Brenchley Gardens. Its frontage faces Museum Street and is adjacent to old houses and cottages. The general atmosphere is fairly quiet. The museum was, as far as I can ascertain, built in the seventeenth century. The Baxter Print Room, in the museum, is a large, clean, well-lighted place.

'I first became aware that there was something peculiar about the Baxter Print Room when I made my first visit there in 1935. I was amazed at the beauty of the works and found great enjoyment, going from picture to picture, in such a collection of exquisite colour and colour tones.

'But gradually this happiness faded and I found myself growing depressed. I tried to pull myself together, but the feeling of acute sadness pervaded my whole being. I found tears welling slowly up in my eyes and I had a hard time to stop them flowing down my cheeks. No one else was in the print room at the time, so I dried my eyes, blew my nose, and, it seemed, under some unknown compulsion, quickly left the room.

'In 1937 I thought I would again visit this room and although I wandered and walked all over the building, or so it seemed to me, I could not find the Baxter Room. It is true that I could have enquired as to its whereabouts from any of the attendants but I refrained from doing so as my time was somewhat restricted and I left the museum on this occasion without my object being achieved.

'Once more, in 1938, I tried to personally locate the print room; but as on the previous occasion I failed to locate it and obstinate as I can be, I did not ask an attendant who could have quickly directed me. Early in 1939 I became interested in ghost lore and legend and that year I began my investigations into some of the haunted places in Kent.

'In 1940 I thought it would be a good idea to go to the Baxter Room and see whether I could unravel the mysterious depression I had felt there five years previously — providing I could find the room! I went there in June 1940, found the room immediately, and spent nearly two hours there one afternoon.

'It should be understood that I regarded this investigation as purely experimental in character. There is no record, as far as I know, of psychic phenomena, or even a ghost story, attached to the Baxter Print Room; either regarding the prints themselves or their originator, George Baxter. I merely sought for some sort of explanation for the acutely depressive mood I had experienced on my first visit to this particular part of the museum in 1935.

'It was just two o'clock when I reached the museum and set out to look for the Baxter Room; and I found it almost immediately. Evidently I took all the right turnings this time. So just after two o'clock I was happily inside the print room and I stayed in the room for nearly two hours. It was so quiet that I could differentiate between the wing sounds caused by a few kinds of insects humming and blundering around the room and at the windows.

'I began my inspection of the prints in the cases first, lingering over the colour pictures of the Mudie Natural History books. Then I went over to the walls and made lengthy surveys of the various prints hanging there. I was opposite Number 348, "The Day Before Marriage", a print published in 1853 from a painting by Fanny Corbaux, when I turned and a small print nearby caught my eye. The picture was Number 353 and called "The Belle of the Village", a print made in 1854 from the original painting by Louis.

'The bold, challenging eyes of the buxom rural wench in the harvest field seemed to fascinate me with their hard beauty, and somehow, my thoughts and imagination told me that such boldness coupled with such beauty could well twist the hearts of all types of men; but women of this type, of which she appeared to me to be a symbol, often experienced great unhappiness and extremes of sorrow when the days of their youthful beauty had passed.

'Then, for the first time during that visit and then very slightly, a depressive-mood began to overtake me; an awareness of something sad in the immediate vicinity became apparent to me. My eyes began to water as on the first occasion (five years before) although the depression was only a fraction of what it had been on that former visit and I could not find anything in the atmosphere of "The Belle of the Village" to cause depression. On the 1935 visit the depression had assailed me most forcibly while I was looking at the prints of the Mudie Natural History books, although the "Belle of the Village" was almost opposite to me across the room from the glass-topped cases in which the Mudie book resided. Could the clue be in the Number 348 print?

'I turned and gazed at the deeply thoughtful face of the young woman in "The Day Before Marriage", but the mood had already passed and my eyes were practically dry. Turning, I walked along the wall, stopping from time to time, trying to contact the depressive, spiritless mood, but nothing happened.

'I then seated myself in a chair, at one end of the room, for about twenty minutes. I was nearly the length of the room from the prints Numbers 348 and 353 and about the same distance from the Mudie volumes in the case. I sat and tried steadily to "tune-in" to any form of psychical activity that might be in the room and could have caused the distinct mood of depression or awareness to sorrow; and I found that I was able to "immobilise" myself to the extent that I could concentrate all my thoughts upon the "mood", but nothing happened.

'Then, as my eyes kept turning to where the framed prints (Numbers 348 and 353) hung, I moved over to that corner and again, in a spirit of detachment from all the other prints — or as near as one can get from visual detachment in a known field of consciousness — I tried to find a clue to the mystery. I tried with print Number 348, "The Day Before Marriage", but could not get any repeat of the former mood. Slowly I retraced my steps and walked round the large room, stopping at the case in which lay the Mudie books on Nature, almost opposite print Number 353, "The Belle of the Village".

'Very, very slowly the sadness of spirit or depressive-mood assailed me again, but without the suddenness and the overwhelming heaviness of spirit as on the 1935 first visit. I recalled that it was at this particular spot that I had previously been so swiftly overcome with sadness culminating in tears and a sense of wishing to be quickly quit of the room.

'Moving away, the mood passed off at once on this occasion. Going over to the "Belle of the Village" print I began to concentrate upon it. The mood came back and my eyes began to moisten. Yet it was not from print Number 353 that the mood was picked up, this I felt certain.

'Once again I moved away from this corner of the room and tried to make tears come by concentration and I was able to do so, but it took some fifteen to thirty seconds each time. The mood brought about by the apparent phenomena present in this particular section in the vicinity of prints Numbers 348 and 353 made the tear-ducts work more quickly, perhaps from five to eight seconds, and I found that repeated movements away from this section, a corner section, and then back again proved how much more powerful the mood was in the corner section — certainly more than anywhere else in the room — for the big difference between the two tear methods was the same in this section: phenomena-mood and mental suggestion tears.

'By this time I was almost on the point of giving up, at least for a time, the investigation. I decided to try once more however and, standing opposite print Number 353, the mood again assailed me. Then, glancing down, I noticed a little way below this print, a framed print which immediately struck me very forcibly with its extraordinary beauty and use of colour. It was print Number 354, entitled "Flora, the Gypsy Girl".

'As I drank my mental fill of the loveliness of this life-like print, published in 1852, I felt the mood more and more, and yet I now discovered that it was not really a moody-sadness or feeling of depression, but rather a quiet peace of mind linked with past times, a sense of things passed away, as if someone had enjoyed the full bounties of nature and, passing out of this life, had left behind a nucleus of a dominating mood that could align or affect a living person many years later.

'Who then might "Flora, the Gypsy Girl" have been? The question seemed as good as answered by a note attached to the frame: " . . . Said to be a portrait of Baxter's daughter, 1852". Would this account for the phenomena I had experienced?

'I discovered that George Baxter had worked hard, for ever trying to improve on his wonderful processes, until between *1850 and 1854* he seemed to become inspired and his work became so life-like, so gloriously and colourfully alive, that some of the portraits seem to have breath and being — suspended as if for a moment — ready to speak, laugh, cry or scold.'

Summing up his experiences in the Baxter Print Room, Frederick Sanders felt that the depressive feeling could have been largely self-induced since he had always felt much sympathy for Victorian art; and yet there was another possibility: the survival of a mood. He wondered whether the conscious part of the mind could continue to exist after the death of the physical body. If the conscious can survive, perhaps it could be broken up into different parts; possibly, if this is the case, the lesser or recessive parts might fade and cease to exist, leaving only the greater or more dominant parts as nuclei . . . or does some special part or nucleus of the whole consciousness survive, the final super-dominant, which might have been acquired throughout life and is really what might be termed the 'life time acquired full personality of the living mind'? If such a surviving mood or super-dominant nucleus continues to exist, then perhaps under special conditions, it might be stimulated by a corresponding mood emanating from a living, fully conscious mind, and so affect that living mind that 'phenomena' such as he experienced could result. Why, if this should be so, it should exist in respect of some of the prints that are housed in the Baxter Print Room and not anywhere else, he cannot imagine, unless it does exist elsewhere and is associated with the receptive, artistic type of person who is to a greater or lesser degree affected by works of art. It is a question that calls out for study and investigation.

## Margate

The Theatre Royal, now sadly a bingo hall, has been described as southern England's most haunted theatre: a multi-haunted place. I remember it as a big theatre (it seated about two thousand people), full of atmosphere, but I did not see the ghost in one of the boxes — a ghost that is said to draw back the curtains if they are closed — that Macqueen Pope told me he saw. Nor did I see the ball of orange light or hear the mysterious sounds of whispering, the inexplicable footsteps or the thuds and thumps and bangs that have convinced many people that this historic building is indeed haunted.

Margate's theatre was opened in 1874 and many famous actors have walked its boards. Under the guidance of one-time actress Sarah Thorne it became the best-known theatre in the south of England but by the turn of the century its fortunes had declined and eventually it became a furniture store. Re-opened as a theatre in 1930, it soon became a cinema, then back to a theatre and then a centre for bingo fans.

Fred Archer, a newspaper editor, first told me about the haunting of the Theatre Royal which, he said, dated from 1918 when the ghost of Sarah Thorne was first seen. Over the succeeding years her ghost has been reported to revisit the theatre she loved, perhaps in protest at the uses to which the place has been put. Fred Archer said he had talked with eight people, from varied walks of life, who had seen the ghost of a woman, presumably Sarah Thorne, in the theatre over a period of twenty years, and at the time they encountered the ghost none of them had any idea that the theatre was reputed to be haunted. Among other arresting phenomena reported he told me about an orange-coloured ball of light that moved across the stage; a scream that seems to begin back-stage and then travel across the stage, through the theatre and out of the stage door; and of course the mysterious ghost in the theatre box.

Macqueen Pope, who was no stranger to ghosts and had seen for himself the famous Man in Grey at his beloved Drury Lane Theatre, said he believed this partial ghost was that of an actor who had committed suicide by throwing himself from the theatre box into the orchestra pit in the early 1900s. Joseph Braddock, a perceptive investigator, told me he had reason to believe the suicide took place in late Georgian or early Victorian days when there were still stock companies. An actor in one of them had been dismissed, he believed unjustly, and he threw himself from the box the following night. Soon the ghostly form of a man was reported to be seen sitting motionless in the fatal box and when such reports became numerous and troublesome the manager withdrew the box from sale, leaving it permanently curtained and then the ghost got into the habit of drawing back the curtains and so, finally, the haunted box was bricked-up.

Later stories of curious happenings at the theatre include a spate of disturbances in 1955, another in 1966 and again in 1972. Howard Lee was an assistant stage manager in January 1955 and he spoke of the heavy front doors of the theatre repeatedly becoming unbolted by themselves, sometimes twice within a few hours; of the foyer lights blazing for hours after they had been put out; of the eerie sound of whispering from the empty stage; of a curious ball of light appearing in the theatre; and of a sensation of unease that was almost overwhelming.

In January 1964 two chorus girls were convinced that they saw a ghost on stage during a late-night rehearsal. One fainted and the other had to be helped from the stage and given time to recover.

In January 1966 Alfred Tanner was working on the restoration and redecoration of the theatre. At that time the building was being used during the daytime for bingo so Tanner did most of his work by night. At first all went well and he worked quite happily in the deserted theatre through most of one night but during the following night he was astonished to hear a series of sounds coming from the stage. He stopped work and went to see what was going on. As he approached the stage the sounds ceased but as he left it they began again and he listened intently, completely mystified. It was just as though someone or possibly two people were whispering so that the words were just inaudible. Eventually he tried to ignore it and resumed his work. Then he heard the creak of floorboards, and he might have ignored that, but when he heard the distinct sound of footsteps moving towards him from behind, and very close, he could no longer disregard what was happening.

He turned round to see who was there and the footsteps ceased instantly. There was nothing to be seen. Then he heard a door bang to, violently; he thought it sounded like the door of the box office. He hurried out of the auditorium but again he found nothing to account for the sounds and there was no sign of anybody else anywhere in the theatre.

Alfred Tanner pulled himself together, told himself he must be imagining things and what he was hearing were natural sounds in an empty theatre at night. He resumed his work and then he heard the footsteps again. They were approaching him from behind, exactly as he had heard them previously. This time he decided he would not turn round but he would wait and see what might happen. The footsteps seemed to approach within inches of him and then they stopped. The hair on the back of his neck was pricking as he suddenly turned round. There was nothing to be seen but as he turned a heavy thud sounded on the floor of the auditorium, between the front row of the stalls and the stage; it sounded for all the world as though a heavy object had fallen from the ceiling to the floor but there was nothing to be seen that might account for the noise — and yet, as Alfred Tanner looked about him, he saw dust rising from the floor, just as it might if a real object had fallen. Raymond Lamond Brown, writing about this incident in his *Phantoms of the Theatre* (1978) makes the intriguing point: 'could this have been the materialised impact of the ghostly suicide's cadaver hitting the floor?'

The next night Alfred Tanner was again disturbed as he worked at restoring the vanishing glory of the Theatre Royal. This time he saw the coloured ball of light long associated with the haunted theatre. He said at the time it was a 'semi-transparent globular object measuring about ten inches across' and it moved across the stage; then the ball seemed to form into the shape of a head and then, to Tanner's relief, it disappeared. As he turned Alfred Tanner saw, without a shadow of a doubt he said, the curtains by the exit door move as though someone was about to pass through them.

The following night Alfred Tanner took his assistant, Lawrence Rodgers, with him to the theatre, having only said that he would like to get a particular piece of work finished quickly. When both men heard a loud bang from the direction of the dress circle, Lawrence Rodgers investigated at once but could find no reason or cause for the sound. Alfred Tanner now reported everything he had experienced to the management and they informed the police. The following night the police called at the theatre and made a number of enquiries and satisfied themselves that there were no intruders in the theatre.

In January 1972 another man working on some paintwork at the Theatre Royal heard sounds he could not account for and saw what he thought was a ball of light cross the theatre. He was so upset that he knocked over a tin of paint in his hurry to get out of the theatre!

Odd that so many of the strange experiences at the Theatre Royal, Margate, have apparently taken place during the month of January; perhaps that was the month of the suicide or maybe there is something about the theatre at that time that is conducive to cyclic phenomena.

## Meopham

What has been described as 'probably the most successful and certainly the most interesting broadcast of a psychic nature' was relayed from the old haunted house known as Dean Manor by the BBC in 1936.

Harry Price told the story in his *Fifty Years of Psychical Research* (1939) where he states that the house, parts of which are hundreds of years old, belonged at that time to a friend of his and the idea was to give listeners, for the first time, an idea of the technique employed in investigating an allegedly haunted house and an accompanying photograph (courtesy of *The Times*) shows him seated at a table before the great fireplace and in front of him, in addition to a BBC microphone, various electrical instruments and paraphernalia which would automatically indicate any abnormal happening such as variation in temperature, in various parts of the house.

Before conducting the experiment Harry Price had been informed, by a previous occupant, Mr G. Varley, that during the six months he had lived at Dean Manor, in 1931 and 1932, he had seen the ghost on several occasions. Once he was so terrified that he threw a poker at the form — which had no effect! Mr Varley believed the house to be haunted by more than one ghost and was especially irritated by the apparently paranormal opening of the cellar door. No matter how often he closed the door, usually several times a day, it was always open again as soon as he turned his back.

Harry Price, with his considerable experience of ghost hunting, did not really expect to broadcast any actual phenomena and he pointed out that it is nearly always the case in haunted houses that such happenings are 'so very spontaneous, rare and sporadic'. Yet, one phenomenon did apparently occur!

The sensitive transmitting thermograph had been in the 'haunted cellar' all day and the temperature was quite constant, as shown by the straight line of the graph across the chart. However, at 9.45 p.m., during the broadcast, the temperature suddenly rose slightly, and then fell sharply below anything that had been measured during the day. 'This kick in the graph could not be accounted for in terms of normality', states Harry Price.

He ends his report: 'If we heard nothing unusual during the broadcast, it was certainly not the fault of Mr S.J. de Lotbiniére, BBC Director of Outside Broadcasts, who was in charge of the transmission; or of myself, who set a number of traps for the ghost. But certain of those present at the broadcast slept in the house that night and one at least heard footsteps in the early hours which could not be accounted for. The only thrill I received that evening was the finding of a human thigh bone, much the worse for post-mortem wear, which some humorist had placed in my car during the broadcast.'

Ten years ago I tried to persuade the then owners to allow a few Ghost Club members to call briefly at Dean Manor, after hearing reports of the ghost of a servant girl being seen there and in view of the interesting psychic history of

Harry Price making his historic broadcast from the 'haunted manor' at Meopham in 1936. (Photo: *The Times* and Harry Price Library, University of London)

the place, but the occupant at that time did not wish his family to be disturbed and so we did not visit the old haunted manor.

My friend Frederick Sanders encountered much the same attitude in 1939 when he contacted the owner at that time, Mr Barry-Thomas, who said in his reply: 'I very much regret that I cannot under any circumstances grant permission for you to conduct any investigations at Dean Manor. Unfortunately, I experienced a great deal of unwelcome publicity which still continues to give me the utmost inconvenience . . .'; however, persistent Frederick Sanders went to view the manor and grounds and managed to get into conversation with the caretaker (named Price!) who stated that he had never seen, heard or felt anything of a supernatural nature at the manor and he scorned the story of a suicide by hanging of a young woman in a barn near the manor; a former granary, already little more than a ruin, near the pond. But nevertheless determined Frederick Sanders decided to carry out an individual on-the-spot investigation in the ruined granary.

The story about the servant girl who hanged herself from a beam in this granary inferred that she had been falsely accused by her mistress of stealing a gold sovereign and this unfair stain on her character, together with an unhappy love affair, preyed on the maid's mind and in a state of mental anguish, she took her own life. Her ghost was said to haunt the scene of her death and the house and grounds. Sanders also traced reports of a sound of axe-blows being heard at the manor for which no explanation could be found, and also occasional tappings and knockings on the doors of the manor and he discovered confirmatory evidence of the opening by itself of a door leading off a passageway giving access to the cellar; no matter how securely the door was closed.

Having decided on his course of action Frederick Sanders carefully noted the hills rising on either side of the manor and grounds and made careful study of the roads and footpaths and landmarks. A month later, during the middle of May, he set out alone to watch at the haunted barn.

He reached the outskirts of the manor about ten o'clock in the evening and the haunted manor was all in darkness by ten-thirty. He had made his way to what remained of the granary which was roughly fifty yards from the rear of the house and from his vantage point he could see the manor, the several outbuildings, the yard and the end of the carriage-way.

Suddenly at 11.10 p.m. he heard, from the direction of the house, a single sound resembling an axe-stroke; it seemed to come from below ground level. One minute later he heard the sounds of a person walking or slouching nearby. The sounds, like footsteps on gravel, came from his right-hand side and out of his line of vision, seemingly somewhere on the gravelly-textured carriageway. At intervals these sounds ceased and then, after a short period, recommenced. Sometimes they appeared to come from beyond the pond and at other times from somewhere near the front of the house; then again they would seem to come from the farther side of the drive, before receding into or recommencing from the top part of the drive. These sounds continued intermittently until 11.15 p.m.

A moment later the peculiar axe-like noise was heard again, once. Three minutes later he heard it again, once only. It did seem to come from the direction of the house, he decided, and yet it appeared to be muffled as though by distance and as before he thought it originated from below ground level.

At 11.21 p.m. he heard the distinct sound of footsteps from approximately fifteen yards to his right, from the other side of the pond or near the edge of the carriageway; he could hear light, dry twigs snap under pressure. The sounds moved away in the direction of the manor and ceased at 11.23 p.m.

At 11.25 p.m. he heard the axe-like sound again. This time it seemed heavier and sharper than before and seemed to come from high rising ground beyond the manor and yet to be of subterranean origin — again there was only one instance of the sound.

At 11.30 p.m. he heard a distinct metallic 'click' from the direction of the back of the house and he decided the sound must have come from a door leading into the small room at the back of the manor. Yet the door, plainly visible to him, did not open or close. The sound was exactly as might be expected had a latch been pressed downwards rather hard in order to release the catch. At the house all appeared to be quiet. At 11.40 p.m. the peculiar axe-like sound was heard yet again — just once.

At 11.45 p.m. he heard footsteps again; this time they moved from one point to another and back again; almost like someone searching for something, all within an area of perhaps fifty square yards. This time the footsteps continued on and off for five minutes. At 11.50 p.m. one more instance of the axe-like sound.

At 11.58 p.m. an ear-piercing cry rent the still, cold air within a few yards of the granary, in the bushes around the pond; and again, and again, and again — terrible cries. Then a scuffling sound and one further sharp, more subdued cry of pain. For a moment the watcher felt alarmed and then a large owl rose out of the rushes by the pond, in its talons a large bird, a thrush or perhaps a blackbird. It winged its way across the valley, the captured bird's cries growing fainter and fainter. Frederick Sanders ended his surreptitious vigil at Dean Manor just after midnight, certain that all the sounds he had heard had a natural explanation, but there are other reported ghosts at Meopham.

The ghost of a headless man is reputed to walk between the Georgian public house and the village church, a few hundred yards away across the road. The path taken by the ghost passes between two pillars but whether these have any significance for the headless apparition or indeed why the monkish figure is headless and why he walks no one seems to know. A resident of Meopham tells me that the figure has been seen within the last few years. Steel Lane is reputedly haunted by the ghost of one Mlle Pinard, the mistress of a soldier of the Napoleonic wars, who hanged herself when she was rejected, dressed in orange silk, and the ghost walks attired in the same startling colour.

## Minster in Thanet

Nearby Cleve Court, part Georgian and part Elizabethan, was very haunted at one time but the manifestations seem to have ceased since the house has been much altered and divided. However there is good evidence that the house was haunted for upwards of sixty years. The pleasant, ten-bedroomed, country house was bought by lawyer and politician Sir Edward Carson in 1920. A great advocate, he is particularly remembered for his merciless cross-examination of Oscar Wilde in 1895. On becoming a lord of appeal in 1921, he was given a life peerage. He died at Cleve Court in 1935 and his body was taken to Belfast for a State funeral. Lady Carson, who often told me how she loved the house from the first time she saw it, lived on at Cleve Court until she died there in 1966.

Lady Carson was as clear-sighted and practical a person as anyone I have met and she was utterly convinced that Cleve Court was haunted. There were the noises at night-time, though never during the day: footsteps that sounded like a woman wearing high heels; taps on doors, as though someone were seeking admission; dragging sounds that disturbed visitors; noises of drawers being opened and closed although nothing physical was ever interfered with. Lord Carson tended to dismiss the curious noises but there were occasions when even he was quite mystified. The time, for example, when Lord and Lady Carson were in their bedroom and a light knock sounded on the door. He called out, 'Come in', but no one did and there was nobody outside; the Carsons were alone in the house at the time.

Soon after they moved into the house an old man in the village told them that a previous owner, many years before, had been a tyrant who kept his wife locked up. She finally died, childless, although her greatest wish had been to have a son or a daughter. It was soon after they heard this story — to which they did not pay much attention — that the Carsons began to notice that whenever children were in the house, a mysterious 'grey lady' was often seen. Patricia Miller, a great niece of Lord Carson, asked her mother who the lady was who stood by her bed — a lady she had seen before, to whom nobody ever talked. This room became known as the 'ghost room' and according to Lady Carson, dogs would not enter it at that time, and she was once amused at finding a servant going to the room at night to carry out some duty there — escorted by another servant who was armed with a broom!

Another child visitor at this time was Joanna Wilson. When she was only eight years old, on a return visit to Cleve Court, she wanted to know whether the lady was still at the house, the lady who 'walks in and out of rooms and nobody speaks to'. A grandson, Rory Carson, visited the house when he was fifteen in 1965 but refused to sleep in the old part of the house . . . a large dog could never be persuaded to stay in the room, either.

It was soon after Lady Carson herself saw the 'grey lady' in 1949 that I first met her and she told me of her experiences. She had been awakened about one-thirty a.m. by her spaniel, Susan, who needed to be let out. Lady Carson put on a dressing-gown and, leaving a light on the landing by her bedroom, took the dog downstairs. As she passed a switch on the stairs she accidentally turned the light off but continued down the stairs and stood waiting for Susan to return indoors. When she did so the dog immediately began to run back up the stairs, then suddenly stopped dead in its tracks. Lady Carson switched on the lights and found the dog whimpering and shivering and looking up the stairs.

There, on the landing, a grey-coloured lady was floating noiselessly down towards them. When the figure reached a half-landing, it turned and disappeared through an open door into the old part of the house. Lady Carson described the figure minutely. Although she could not see the face clearly, she was certain that it was a young woman who wore a very full grey dress that reached to her feet, a pale grey lace cape on her neck and shoulders, and a white ribbon in her hair. The form appeared to be quite solid but Lady Carson knew by the silence and by the behaviour of her dog that she was seeing a ghost and she was terrified. She told me she had never been so frightened of anything in her life; she felt ice-cold and began to shiver until the figure disappeared from sight.

After reports of Lady Carson's experience appeared in print a former house-maid at Cleve Court wrote to her. The latter related that when she was fifteen years old, she had been busy early one morning in the old part of the house when she heard footsteps coming along the passage. She had looked up, expecting to see one of the other maids but saw instead a lady in an 'old-fashioned dress'. As the girl got up and prepared to leave the room, the 'grey lady' waved a hand and went away.

The Hon. Edward Carson, a former Member of Parliament and Lord and Lady Carson's only son, was hardly a year old when the family moved to Cleve Court and when he was six he told his mother that he did not like the lady who walked in the passage outside his room. Lady Carson, who knew this could be no 'normal' lady, asked her son what she looked like. 'I don't know', little Edward replied. 'I've only seen her walking away'. Some years ago Mrs Edward Carson heard footsteps approaching down a passage as she came out of a bathroom. The footsteps seemed to pass her, although she saw nothing. This was the same year that Lady Carson saw the 'grey lady'. She used to say that the apparition was never seen again and footsteps were never heard after that night, but an ex-hospital sister, who knew nothing of the ghost of Cleve Court, told me that she too heard footsteps pass her bedroom very late at night; and there is other evidence that the phenomenon of unexplained footsteps continued well after Lady Carson's death.

My friend Andrew MacKenzie of the Society of Psychical Research has conducted a long investigation into the haunting of Cleve Court and he has written about the case in the Journal of the S.P.R. and in his books, *The Unexplained* (1966) and *Hauntings and Apparitions* (1982). Lady Carson told him that a year after they bought Cleve Court a guest sleeping in the Elizabethan part had a restless night, being disturbed by sounds overhead of something being dragged about and of drawers being opened and shut. In the morning she asked Lady Carson if the sounds were made by a footman packing before leaving. Lady Carson knew, however, that there was no bedroom above the guest room, that no servant was leaving, and that servants did not sleep in that part of the house.

Lady Carson also told Andrew MacKenzie about the strange experience that befell Dr E.G. Moon. He had been asked to call on Lord Carson one day in 1930 and, after attending to his patient, the doctor paused at the front door, half-wondering whether he should have prescribed a different tonic. When he looked up he saw a totally different scene from that which had been there when he arrived. His car had vanished, as had the thick hedge situated between two sets of gateposts and instead of the lane which he had just driven down there appeared only a muddy cart track. Coming towards him was a man who was wearing a caped coat, top hat, and gaiters at which he flicked noiselessly with a hunting crop.

The man seemed to stare at Dr Moon who, hardly believing what he was seeing, decided to go back into the house. Then he decided to have another look at the odd stranger — and what he then saw was his car where he had left it and the scenery of the present day restored. Of the man who had stared so intently at him, there was no sign.

The identity of the 'grey lady' has never been definitely established but it seems likely that the unhappy and childless wife of the tyrant who once lived at Cleve Court is a strong contestant. Certainly such a legend, an heiress who was unhappily married, has been circulating in the neighbourhood of Cleve Court for nearly two hundred years.

In his fascinating *Rooms of Mystery and Romance* (1931) Allan Fea mentions the ghost of an aged monk that usually put in an appearance at the Old Oak Cottage at Minster, during the month of September, although he 'is not over particular about the date'. Fea tells us that this ancient building is thought to have been a guest house attached to St Mildred's Abbey and the ghostly old gentlemen, when he turns up, is treated 'more as a guest than a ghost' both for old times sake and because the 'dear old thing' (as the lady of the house at the time called him) evidently means no harm and does not even cause alarm.

Apparently the cottage used to be divided into separate tenements and then the cowled monastic visitor did not put in an appearance. It was only after some of the original oak beams had been exposed to view and some of the original windows reinstated that he walked again. According to Fea this ghost monk has been seen in daylight as well as night-time (when the figure seems to be lit by an ethereal light) and although he has been seen in various parts of the premises, he does seem to show a preference for one snug little bedroom that 'shows marked evidence of its venerable age'. Once a lady sleeping in this room awakened to hear the shuffling of sandals in the passage outside; 'then a bright light appeared and with it the shadowy outline of a hooded figure . . . '

## Pembury

Well over a hundred years ago now there died, at Old Bayhall Manor, a certain Anne West, the last mistress, worthy of mention, of this ancient fortified manor house that was once the residence of some well-known families: the Colpeppers, the Duke of Buckingham, and the Amhersts who were responsible for six Almhouses at Pembury. An early eighteenth century engraving shows a grand mansion set amid extensive and well-laid-out grounds, of which only the fish pond is recognisable today.

In common with many educated people of her day Anne West was always worried that she might be buried while yet alive. She thought that although she might appear to be dead, to her doctor and everyone else, she might in fact be in a coma of suspended animation and it terrified her to think that she might wake out of such a state to find herself buried . . . so she inserted a clause in her will to the effect that she was to be placed, after her death, in an open tomb or small individual vault, above ground in the churchyard of Pembury Old Church, a mile or so from her home. The vault was to be covered with a 'box' or 'tabletomb', four-sided with a heavy flat top and at one end, the east side, a grille was

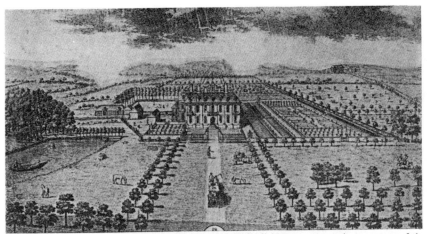

An eighteenth century drawing of extensive Old Bayhall Manor; now only remnants of the fishpond remain

to be inserted and so constructed that it could be opened from inside the vault. The coffin, resting on a low support, was to have its lid left unscrewed and over the face of the body a small window was to be inserted in the coffin-lid.

Furthermore Anne West's bailiff was to be instructed to bring to the vault, each evening just before sunset, a basket of food and a flask of wine, and these victuals were to be placed near the grille where, should she awaken, she would be able to reach them and also summon help from any passer-by. This practice was to be continued for one year after her burial.

These instructions were duly carried out to the letter — for about a month after Anne West was buried and then, suddenly and mysteriously, the bailiff disappeared from the district and was never again located although rumour had it that he had emigrated to Australia. Rumour also said that he profited handsomely from his position in the West household and that for years he had systematically robbed his former mistress and after her death he staged a quiet and well-planned exodus from the Pembury district and from the law.

Not surprisingly perhaps the churchyard of Pembury Old Church is or was reputedly haunted by the ghost of Anne West and her untrustworthy bailiff. From Old Bayhall Manor, along the lonely cart track and carriage road until it reaches the village main road, the ghostly figure of the bailiff is said to walk. The restless phantom form is also supposed to roam at night among the fields and roads surrounding the old estate. Anne West died in the 1830s aged thirty-seven years.

Writing some forty years ago Frederick Sanders describes Old Bayhall as a derelict manor; the main outer walls were some six feet thick and almost certainly there were secret passages within the walls, while under the house extensive cellars had been securely blocked-up. 'At night' he writes, 'this ruinous edifice

The one-time fish pond of Old Bayhall Manor, Pembury.

presents itself as an "eerie pile"; it lies in a valley, surrounded by wooded hills, and near the manor, in the grounds, stood a large sheet of water, once a lake. The banks and water are in a deplorable condition; weeds and rushes choking the banks: the haunt of water vole, mallard and moorhen. The ruined manor is alive with the scurrying and squeaking of rats while the monotonous sound of water dripping into one of the old blocked-up cellars adds to the eerieness of the place. From time to time sounds of movement that might be thought to be human beings are caused by rabbits in the long grass or moving over the broken surfaces of stones and rubble in the vicinity of this once-haunted place . . . '

Frederick Sanders decided to spend a night in the area and he did so one February, accompanied by Kenneth Jefferey, a Rover Scout and out-of-doors man who had little or no belief in anything of a supernormal nature.

From nine o'clock until ten-thirty that evening the ghost watchers spent wandering among the ruins of Old Bayhall and they saw nothing unusual during that time and heard only the normal sounds of night in such a place: water voles chewing aquatic plants, ducks and moorhens disturbed, the movements of rats and rabbits and the piping of bats. They left the ruins and walked along the allegedly haunted old cart road from the manor to the village and again experienced nothing untoward.

They made their way to Pembury Old Church and stationed themselves inside the churchyard from soon after eleven o'clock and stayed there until about half-an-hour after midnight. They illuminated the interior of Anne West's open vault by directing the beam of a torch downwards through the small grille and they could make out the crumbled remnants of the coffin and the remains of Anne West herself. 'Her skull', Frederick Sanders told me, 'lay upon the floor of the tomb, minus the lower jaw . . . '

At half-an-hour to midnight Sanders placed his self-illuminating watch on the flat top of the tomb just above the position of the grille. 'A sudden drop in temperature of psychic origin might quite possibly stop the watch, as sudden extremes of cold are apt to affect the delicate mechanisms of watches and clocks', he pointed out. 'Also, if there happened to be any poltergeistic influence around the watch might get moved, dropped or flung about . . . ' His report continues:

'As we stood silently near the old tomb a noise like a subdued rustling became audible, followed by a light thump, followed again by a jerking, gritty sound. Turning, we glimpsed a small black form bounding along the pathway. It was a black cat at full gallop and it quickly disappeared into the gloom on the further side of the graveyard. We then gradually became aware of a light, almost phosphorescent, glow suffusing the south side of the church at short irregular intervals. This, we discovered, was caused by the light from the moon high up in the night sky shining through the ragged gaps in the broken waves of storm clouds passing overhead at a height of about two thousand feet.

'Just before 11.40 p.m. my co-watcher went over to the church porch and went inside to get out of the cold, damp, and windy atmosphere; he did not seem at all hopeful about seeing anything. Meanwhile I moved nearer the tomb where I could hear my watch ticking, very faintly, and I then stationed myself in the centre of the church path where I was almost within touching distance of the watch.

'At approximately 11.40 p.m. I felt three taps upon my right shoulder; it felt just as though someone behind me had touched me with their finger ends or the tip of a light stick, as if to say: stand aside please. I turned at once: there was no one there. I turned my face to the sky and wind: no drops of rain were falling. I could see nothing on my shoulder and I was wearing a light-coloured raincoat at the time. There were no bushes or trees with overhanging branches from which droplets of accumulated moisture could have fallen anywhere near me. Kenneth Jefferey came quickly from the church porch at my call. I asked him to shine his torch on my right shoulder to look for a mark or any sign of moisture. He did so and found nothing. Then to make sure I divested myself of the raincoat and made a scrupulous examination. I could find no clue to the three taps. Ten minutes later I placed the watch as near as I could to the grille and both of us stood on the grass at the end of the tomb and kept our eyes fixed on the watch. For ten minutes nothing happened. I replaced the watch in my coat pocket and shortly afterwards we left the area.'

Later Frederick Sanders added the following 'Remarks' to his Report:

'I consider that this investigation was highly successful: the super-nature of the three taps seemed to be established and I believe they were of quasi-sensory origin . . . Kenneth Jefferey took home a tile and a piece of partially rotted beam from the Old Bayhall Manor rubble as souvenirs. For future experimentation I retained from Old Bayhall a piece of iron work, evidently from a door, that might be of use to anyone interested in the practice of psychometry.'

Visiting the site of Old Bayhall Manor, through the courtesy of farmer and landowner M.L.J. Bowman, in May 1984, I found that a large barn now stands where once the property known as 'The Haunted House' had stood and only a few fragmentary remains were distinguishable as stones from the old house and of course there is still the former fish pond. I found too that the grille in Anne West's tomb had been bricked-up and so perhaps yet another Kentish ghost has been laid to rest.

## Penshurst

'Everywhere about is that haunting beauty which makes our countryside the envy of the world,' wrote Arthur Mee, describing Penshurst, and this is a lovely spot. The village is rich in timbered houses; there is a bricked court enclosed on three sides by ancient houses with overhanging upper storeys; there is a church that dates from 1200; a line of limes centuries old; and to crown it all there is incomparable Penshurst Place.

Here is the finest baronial hall in England where Henry VIII feasted and Elizabeth I danced with her favourite Robert Dudley, Earl of Leicester. James I knew Penshurst; and the Black Prince dined here with his Fair Maid of Kent; and under the oaks in the huge park the children of Charles I walked, sent here by Cromwell to be looked after when they were fatherless. But it is another boy who walked about this place a hundred years earlier who is forever associated with Penshurst Place, the great Sir Philip Sidney who was born here and whose spirit seems to linger in every part of this beautiful house. Indeed his ghost has long been reputed to walk here although he was buried in St Paul's Cathedral and his tomb perished in the Great Fire of London; not that that has any bearing on where his ghost may be seen. His heart and mind were always fixed on Penshurst and if his ghost walks anywhere, it is meet and right that it should walk at Penshurst Place; and yet the evidence is scanty.

Joan Forman, in her book *The Haunted South* (1978) relates the experience of a lady from East Worthing who visited Penshurst Place with some relatives and while they were walking up a flight of stone steps the lady perceived someone descending, a woman wearing Elizabethan costume complete with ruff and farthingale . . . the visitor attempted to draw the attention of her companions to the brilliant figure but they were totally unable to see the form.

Similar stories are told of many reputedly haunted houses and one either accepts that such apparitions are only perceivable to certain people or that the forms have in fact no objective reality outside the mind or brain of the person who believes she sees them.

The nearby rectory, where limes stand in the quiet garden, has a ghost story that tells of a long ago love affair between the daughter of a former man of God here and a young man with few prospects who was regarded as a quite unsuitable match for the headstrong young girl who proceeded to meet her lover secretly.

At twilight he would steal across the lane and wait for his love. No one now knows what became of the affair or what happened to either of the couple but the ghostly figure of an unidentified man in old-fashioned clothes has been glimpsed from time to time, surreptitiously making his way across the lawn and towards the house: some psychic fragment of a passion-laden episode perhaps that has been forgiven and forgotten long, long ago.

## Plaxtol

Near this unspoilt place, Old Soar Manor, which once belonged to a knight in the reign of Edward I, is a remarkable survival of thirteenth century domestic architecture; but its ghostly associations seem to originate in the eighteenth century.

The mediaeval parts of the property, open to the public, include a solar, a chapel and a room with a garderobe, all dating from about 1290. The solar, once the living room of the lord of the manor, stands on a barrel-vaulted undercroft. Attached is the eighteenth century brick farmhouse built on the foundations of an aisled hall dating back some five hundred years before the farmhouse was built; a hall that was destroyed by fire more than three hundred years ago.

Old Soar (Norman for 'grief') once belonged to the famous Colpeppers of Preston, at the time when the Colpeppers where the largest landowners in Kent and Sussex; a state of affairs that reputedly came about through the family's habit of kidnapping heiresses and forcing them to marry a Colpepper!

Later the property passed to the Geary family and, according to tradition, some two hundred years ago a young dairymaid was seduced by a young family priest. When she became pregnant some sort of altercation took place in the chapel and the girl fell or was knocked unconscious and was found face down in the piscina, having drowned in a couple of inches of water. The Geary family decided that the death had been one of suicide and the girl's body was buried at midnight in unconsecrated ground.

A couple of hundred years later, in 1971, a local resident told a new caretaker at Old Soar that the building had long been haunted by the ghost of an eighteenth century dairymaid who had committed suicide — or been murdered — in the chapel after becoming pregnant by a priest. For the first time the caretaker then heard stories of a ghostly young girl walking in the chapel; of moving lights being seen in the empty building; of the sound of music emanating from the dark and deserted chapel — this 'church music' even being heard by the occupants of the adjoining farmhouse, seemingly issuing through the intervening wall, much to the puzzlement of the people concerned who were under the impression that the old house was empty — as indeed it was, at least of human beings . . .

Visitors to Old Soar have, on occasions, asked whether there is a ghost in the chapel. Some of them have reported 'cold and ghostly feelings' and 'a sudden coldness' for which they have been unable to find any explanation. One caretaker, who must have been familiar with the atmosphere and feeling of the place, said that he sometimes found himself affected by the feeling of 'an unhappy presence' in the vicinity of a spiral staircase. And a local man is among those who have reported hearing the unmistakable sound of footsteps passing through or pacing an empty room; most frequently it seems this apparent phenomenon occurs during the month of June.


## Pluckley

According to Jack Hallam and his *Ghost Tour* (1967) this charming village has more ghosts than any other village in Kent and is 'very near the top of the league table for the most haunted village in England'. Andrew Green, in his *Shire Album of Haunted Houses* (1975) refers to it as the 'most haunted village of Britain'. Whatever the truth of such claims Pluckley has become something of a Mecca for ghost hunters and it would seem that about a dozen ghosts haunt or have haunted the immediate area. When the Ghost Club visited Pluckley in 1976 we visited the allegedly haunted sites and talked with people who had seen the ghosts.

Some of the more acceptable hauntings are connected with the Dering family who came to Pluckley many centuries ago; John Dering died here in 1425 and there were Derings at Pluckley until the Great War of 1914-1918. Unfortunately Sir Edward Dering (1599-1644) 'restored' many of the family brasses in the thirteenth century church and it seems certain that on occasions he falsified names and dates, since, according to Arthur Mee, 'he was not above a little forgery for the aggrandisement of his family'. Nevertheless the Derings were undoubtedly rewarded by the Crown for their loyalty and there is a story that after the Civil War the Lord Dering of the day was granted as much land thereabouts as he could ride his horse around in a day.

Some of the houses and the village inn, the Black Horse, have windows with curved tops; it was from such a window that Lord Dering eluded capture by the Roundheads on one occasion by diving through it headfirst and when he came to build his manor house he had every window built in this style, in memory of his daring escape. The manor was burned down in 1952 but a ghostly White Lady is said to revisit the site.

The seven-hundred year old Black Horse inn, where furniture has been reported to move by itself, stands in a lane where a schoolmaster hanged himself for some forgotten reason and his ghostly form has been reportedly seen swinging from one of the overhanging trees. At the house next door to the Black Horse Margaret Williamson has twice seen a 'translucent apparition with dark curly hair . . .' Another haunted tree — appropriately at a crossroads called Fright Corner — is the stump of a hollow oak tree where a highwayman made his last stand. Cornered after a chase, he stood with his back against the stout oak and endeavoured to defend himself but he was run through by a sword and pinned to the tree, there to die in agony. On bright moonlit nights this grisly episode is said to be re-enacted by phantom figures that make not a single sound.

The church of St Nicholas, where many of the Dering family lie buried, is haunted by a Lady Dering who died while still young and beautiful. Her grief-stricken husband, wishing to preserve her loveliness, had her dressed in rich apparel with a red rose at her breast, and her body was placed in an air-tight coffin, this coffin being encased in a second and then a third, also of lead. The three coffins were then enclosed in an oaken one and the quadruple casket buried in the family vault, beneath the Dering Chapel. In spite of these encumbrances Lady Dering is said to walk in the churchyard on certain unspecified nights, resplendent in her finery and with a red rose at her breast, the last gift of her lord. This story was for a long time a closely guarded family secret and there have been suggestions that she may have been as wicked as she was beautiful. Unexplained and mysterious lights have also been reported shining through the upper portions of the stained glass windows of the Dering Chapel where eerie knockings have also been heard. One psychic investigator, watching in the church one July night, heard a knocking sound that he could not explain and saw 'splashes of flaming yellow-green light' blazing in the upper-half of the stained glass of the Dering Chapel. The light was also seen by his co-watcher who, twelve minutes later, heard the sounds of a woman's voice in the deserted churchyard.

This sound of a woman's voice, calling in a far-away and pathetic manner, has been reported from the churchyard on many occasions and the ghostly form of a woman in red, known as the Red Lady, has been seen among the gravestones. She is believed to be another member of the Dering family who is searching for her lost baby. A huge white phantom hound also haunts the churchyard and was seen by some students who camped there one Hallowe'en a few years ago.

The Rector, the Rev. John Pittock, who went to Pluckley in 1964, has become convinced that there are good and bad influences at work in the village and he has conducted several exorcisms in former Dering houses. At one the sound of whispering in one room became so frequent and so frightening that he blessed every room in the house and at another all the occupants found something invisible repeatedly tried to push them down the stairs and although Mr Pittock blessed the house and he thought all was well, the family concerned could not stand the disturbances and the atmosphere and eventually moved away from the village. 'One woman says she hears the fife and drums of a Highland Regiment moving around her house,' the Rector told us. 'There are some very hard-headed and sensible people round here who have seen our famous ghosts and I for one believe there is something in it.' At Elvey Farm, for example, it has been reported that objects have moved of their own accord, including a bowl that was thrown to the floor; footsteps have been heard that had no rational explanation and there is, or was, a regular smell that resembled burning wool.

The old ruined mill is haunted by a former miller who walks when the moon is full seeking his lost love; the ghost of a gypsy or watercress woman, huddled in a shawl and smoking a pipe, has been seen by residents and visitors near the crossroads by the little stone bridge on autumn nights; a man who fell to his death down a claypit returns to frighten passers-by with his screams; the figure of a soldier who committed suicide, known as The Colonel, walks through Park Wood on dark and windy nights; and a phantom coach and horses has been heard clattering along the deserted village street on 'certain' nights of the year.

A mellow house named Greystones is reported to have a ghostly monk and a young correspondent, Andrew Jupp, tells me that while he was on holiday he was having a look round the village and came upon Greystones. He had just decided to take a photograph when he saw a monk walking through the trees. He just had time to see that the figure was wearing a brown habit and then it disappeared.

The ghostly watercress woman — or gypsy — is said to have met her death by accidentally setting fire to herself when she fell asleep still smoking her clay pipe and for some years her figure was repeatedly seen; more recently an odd and inexplicable red glow has been seen at the spot where she died, lighting up the area long after the sun has gone down and always when there is no moon.

At the four-hundred year Old Bakery we met Jane and Mike Henderson who seemed to release a localized cold spot when they removed a Victorian fireplace and exposed the original open hearth. 'Even on the hottest day one spot had an icy chill — and then there were the ghostly footsteps in the room above; they go from the door to the fireplace with some regularity and have been heard by several of our visitors as well as ourselves . . .'

Aileen and Jack Beckworth used to hear 'peculiar knockings' from the direction of their fireplace before they made a number of alterations to the cottage. Once Aileen was walking from the kitchen into the main room when she encountered a 'grey shape'; she nearly dropped the tray she was carrying in her surprise, but as she stood there the shape went past her and into the kitchen. She never saw it again. There is also a ghost in the bedroom of Church Gates that occasionally walks from their house, through the wall, into the bathroom of their neighbour's house! Once, of course, the two cottages were one property.

Certainly Pluckley seems to have a considerable number of reported ghosts and it would be interesting to carry out an extended investigation but several attempts that I have made in this direction have run into difficulties.

## Reculver

The Roman Fort here has long been reputed to be haunted by the sounds of a crying baby and there has been extensive speculation as to whether the Romans had buried a baby alive as a sacrifice when building the Fort, a primitive practice which they certainly indulged in on occasions elsewhere in these islands. Could folk memory have been kept alive in the locality for some sixteen hundred years or could the sounds be a genuine case of haunting; the phantom sounds of a murdered babe?

The Fort dates from the third century AD and during the course of excavation at Reculver some years ago no less than eleven skeletons of infants, all only a few weeks old, were brought to light during archaeological digs. Eric Maple, who has been particularly interested in the Reculver story and was instrumental in originating some of the digs, tells me that one skeleton was found at the centre of a wall, another beneath one of the walls, and yet another at one of the corners of a wall.

I understood that reports still occur of people hearing the pathetic sounds of a baby crying in the area where there is also reputed to be a ghostly Exciseman named Gill who has been glimpsed on dark nights doing silent battle with a long-dead smuggler on the edge of Reculver cliff.

# Rochester

For nearly a thousand years the Norman keep of Rochester Castle (the keep itself is locally known as the 'castle') has defied the ravages of time, of battles, and of the elements; and a White Lady ghost has haunted the castle for more than seven hundred years.

Bishop Gundulf designed the castle soon after he came to Rochester in 1077 but the massive and impressive castle itself we owe to William de Corbeil, Archbishop of Canterbury in the reign of Henry I.

On Good Friday, 1264, Simon de Montfort, Earl of Leicester, was beseiging Rochester Castle; among the defenders of the castle was Ralph de Capo, a Crusader, and with him was Lady Blanche de Warrene, his betrothed. In de Montfort's army was Guilbert de Clare, a knight and a rejected suitor of the Lady Blanche. The seige was raised and, while de Capo left the castle to pursue the retreating rebels, de Clare, disguised in a suit of armour resembling de Capo's, entered the castle and seized Lady Blanche who was on the southern battlement watching the flight of the insurgents. Looking back up at the castle, de Capo saw his lady struggling in the hands of a man whom he knew must be an enemy, and renowned archer that he was, he seized a bow from one of his men and fired an arrow at de Clare. The arrow sped true to its mark but glanced off the armour and pierced the breast of Lady Blanche, killing her. So she died at the hand of her lover.

The same night, according to reports, her ghost walked the battlements in a white robe, her raven hair streaming in the breeze, the fatal arrow still embedded in her bosom; and on the anniversary of the tragedy she is still said to haunt the old castle keep, bewailing her sad story. Psychic investigator Frederick Sanders told me that he knew two people who claimed to have seen her on different occasions.

Such is the generally accepted story of the Lady in White who has also been seen in the vicinity of the round tower at the junction of the south and east

Rochester Castle

battlements. Another story, however, says that she was pursued by de Clare around the top of the keep and endeavoured to escape from him by secreting herself within the round tower; but that she was too late to prevent her old suitor from forcing his way in. Clambering to the top, he caught up with her and it was there that de Capo spotted him and shot the fatal arrow. Yet another version of the story suggests that rather than risk capture by de Clare, she threw herself off the top of the round watchtower and so met her death by suicide. At all events there seems little doubt that she died a violent death and it is difficult to dismiss all the odd happenings at Rochester Castle as figments of imagination.

During the course of spending some hours in the precincts of the castle ruins one Good Friday night, Frederick Sanders himself heard light, rustling footsteps swiftly approach him just before midnight. They seemed to commence some thirty feet away and approached to within three feet of where he stood, practically invisible against the grey stone wall. Looking at the spot where the sounds appeared to come from, he saw the leaves covering the ground near the base of the wall move as if under pressure of something invisible. When the sounds were perhaps a yard from him, they ceased, and the leaves were no longer disturbed. He could find no cause for this; there was no wind, and throughout the rest of his vigil the noise and the movement of the leaves did not recur.

The White Lady is said to haunt the ramparts of the castle keep and the Round Tower; the three other corner towers are square; some writers say she walks the battlements and then disappears into the Round Tower which is also known as the Lady Tower.

During the course of one night visit to Rochester Castle in the company of two professional photographers, the castle caretaker and a police sergeant, Frederick Sanders and Mr Scott, one of the photographers, both heard distinct footsteps and the sound of a man's voice as they descended the stone spiral staircase in the North East Tower. On another night visit when, in addition to those on the previous occasion, Frederick Sander's wife was also present; three of the party heard the sound of footsteps descending the same stairway. A few seconds later they again heard footsteps on the stone steps within the tower, below them and apparently approaching them. When the perpetrator of the footsteps seemed to be almost upon them, Sanders switched on his torch: the footsteps ceased instantly and the stairway was completely deserted.

The Old Burial Ground in the castle moat on the east side and opposite the west door of the cathedral is said to be haunted by the ghost of Charles Dickens. He was always fond of this little graveyard, the old burial ground of St Nicholas, and expressed a wish that he be buried there. He was in fact buried in Westminster Abbey but from time to time a white spectre, with features remarkably like those of Dickens, has been seen wandering among the old tombstones, especially around Christmas time. As Frederick Sanders said to me once: 'Dickens's dust and bones may lie in the metropolis of London but it could be that his spirit clings to the gentler surrounds of the Rochester that he loved'. The graveyard is also said to harbour the ghost of a woman who has never been identified; a forlorn figure that is seen at night seemingly searching for the grave she is never destined to find: the unmarked resting place of her only child.

Minor Canon Row is a quiet road south of the cathedral and across an open space stands The Vines. This area is allegedly haunted by the ghost of a monk in a black habit who walks from The Vines and along Minor Canon Row towards the cathedral where the silent form walks through the ancient cloisters and disappears through a door into the cathedral itself — usually around midnight. Another reputed ghost here is that of a young woman hugging a dead baby to her breast. Around her neck there is a hangman's noose. She is said to walk the length of Minor Canon Row and then fade away . . .

Restoration House in the Maidstone Road, a large and pleasant residence facing The Vines, was the model for Satis House in Dickens' *Great Expectations* in which that most singular and love-frustrated lady Miss Havisham lived with the young girl Estella and where Pip used to visit. The house was erected during the reign of Elizabeth I. At midnight, on certain dates, it is said, the ghostly figure of a girl, very beautiful of face and figure, and in white raiment, leaves Restoration House, crosses the road, traverses The Vines (the Monks Vineyard of Dickens' *The Mystery of Edwin Drood*) and then disappears. It is shortly after she quits the house that the Black Monk appears from this building and makes his way to the cathedral.

In Rochester High Street, near the great 'moon-faced' Corn Exchange clock, the ghost of Charles Dickens is said to appear each Christmas Eve; he sets his watch and winds it as the clock points to midnight — and then disappears for another twelve months.

Restoration House, Rochester

The corridors of the Guildhall were long reputed to be haunted by the ghost of an Admiral in eighteenth century uniform. It was thought to be the shade of pompous Admiral Sir Cloudesley Shovell who was associated with the decoration of some of this interesting building. In 1969 the remains of his flagship *Association* were discovered off the Isles of Scilly and since then the Admiral does not seem to have put in an appearance; however some of the staff here say that one door in the building frequently opens by itself: a door that the Admiral often used. And some of the staff, and also visitors, have sensed an 'unseen presence' here.

Several inns in Rochester are said to be haunted. The Cooper's Arms, probably the oldest public house in Kent, has the ghost of a grey-robed monk-like figure that emerges through the wall of the bar and after disappearing leaves behind a cold and clammy atmosphere. Eight hundred years ago the building formed part of an old priory, the brewery, and the ghost is thought to be that of one of the brethren who was walled-up alive for some forgotten sin. This ghost is said to manifest most frequently during the month of November.

The George Inn is also said to be haunted by a ghostly monk; one landlord describing the unexplained figure is that of 'a very old man, on the small side, and always smiling'. This is no misty, vague form however and witnesses who have encountered the phantom form in the cellar (once a church crypt) describe the monk as 'solid looking' and 'quite natural to look at'. One barman claimed that he was about to leave the cellar on one occasion, after changing the beer barrels, when he found that he was totally unable to move: someone invisible, or some thing, was holding him and for some minutes he was powerless to move. Eventually whatever it was released its hold or power and he climbed up the cellar steps — somewhat faster than he usually did!

Blue Bell Hill, near Rochester, is a high point of the North Downs and overlooks a vast expanse of countryside to the south. According to tradition, and to information handed down by word of mouth, a motiveless crime was committed here, a century or more ago, a crime that has left its mark inasmuch as the ghost of the murderer revisits the scene of his crime.

At the top of the hill stands the old Upper Bell Inn and behind there is a meadow or field, fringed by shrub woodland. Here, in this field near the edge of the wood, the alleged murder was committed. The murderer, a butcher who travelled about the district, used to ride a very fine cob, and so, well-known for his equestrian mode of travel, he became known as the 'galloping murderer'.

This butcher, it is said, murdered a young lad or youth, for no apparent reason in the field and there, later, the body was found just inside the wood. Legend has it that the ghost of the murderer, mounted on his phantom steed, continued to visit the scene of the crime for many years. Up to some fifty years ago the story was well known in the countryside around and several attempts were made by groups of Rochester and Chatham people to authenticate the ghost story. Gradually the legend faded with the passing of the years until it became almost forgotten; although it is still remembered by some of the older inhabitants, survivors of the 'ghost hunts', and local historians. The murdered lad became known as 'the Blue Boy' and the place where he met his death, 'Blue Boy Field'. Oddly enough this area has, in recent years, become the centre of a number of alleged sightings of a 'hitch-hiker ghost'.

Stories, invariably second- or third-hand, tell of someone being picked up and given a lift home; on arrival they have disappeared and when the person giving the lift goes to the house to tell the people there what has happened, he or she is told that the person they gave a lift to died, at the spot where they picked up the 'ghost', some months or years ago. This type of ghost story is quite common today and there are many places said to be the haunt of the 'hitch-hiker' ghost; but I have yet to locate an authentic and first-hand incident.

In 1893 the then owner of The Old Hall (certainly one of the oldest houses in Rochester and possibly the one at which Henry VIII waited to greet Anne of Cleves in 1540) Stephen T. Aveling wrote an article about the house in *Scribner's Magazine* and I reproduce what he had to say about the ghost: 'Every stranger looking at the house exclaims, "That house must have a history and a ghost." Many a story has been told of the ghost which has, from time to time, been seen (or is said to have been seen) within its walls, and many a servant has, from fear, refused service in this so-called haunted house.' He then goes on to describe rumbling sounds which at first he was unable to account for but subsequently discovered to be due to water pipes.

A correspondent tells me that she has never forgotten a strange experience she had some years ago at The Old Hall, then the residence of an elderly friend, Miss Shinkwin. She had agreed to allow a party of antiquarians from London to look over the house and as the party was a fairly large one Miss Shinkwin asked my correspondent, Mrs Joan Marks, to take charge of half the group and show them round. Mrs Marks knew the house well and had previously helped to show people round when Miss Shinkwin occasionally opened the property for charity.

Mrs Marks finished her tour before Miss Shinkwin and her party and when her people had left the house Mrs Marks was quite alone, waiting for Miss Shinkwin to join her. She tells me she was not thinking of anything in particular, certainly not about the house or its history, when she was suddenly aware that the air was vibrating with music, a charming sound which she could only describe, somewhat loosely perhaps, as 'a madrigal type of music'.

When Miss Shinkwin joined her, Mrs Marks immediately told her about the sound of music and she replied, in a very matter of fact tone: 'This is the only room where I have ever heard anything . . . '

Mrs Marks then learned that on one occasion Miss Shinkwin had seen the figure of a woman standing at the foot of her bed. She had never seen or experienced anything else at the house except for the sound of light music in the room where Mrs Marks had heard the same sound; music reminiscent of the Tudor age.

## Saltwood

Slaybrook Hall was originally a mediaeval hall house, rectangular, with dragon beams and moulded windows. The main structure dates from the fifteenth century; alterations were made to the house in the sixteenth century and a new section was added at the back in the 1920s.

Among my records I have information that when Mr and Mrs Reginald Hoskins lived at Slaybrook with their three children, they often had the feeling that they were not alone in the house. Their daughter Zoe noticed from time to time the totally inexplicable and very strong aroma of alcohol in her bedroom and on at least one occasion a regiment of Roman soldiers seemed to pass the gate for most of the night, keeping guests and residents awake with the scraping of their boots and the clatter of their swords and tridents — but there was nothing to see. This curious manifestation is thought to have been associated with a bloody Roman battle which took place in nearby fields many centuries ago when the stream that runs through what is now the garden of the house was said to be awash with the blood of the dead . . . Then there is the story of the empty bus stopping outside the gate for an old lady to climb aboard. The driver took her fare and noted her request to stop a short way up the road. He did so but on turning round to remind her to alight; he was amazed to find his bus completely empty. Perhaps she is the same little old lady who has sometimes been seen, dressed in long and flowing robes, on the bridge over the brook in the garden . . . but when I began to research material for this book I discovered that Slaybrook Hall is now owned by Brigadier J.A. Mackenzie, CBE, DSO, MC, and I cannot do

Slaybrook, Saltwood (Brig. J.A. MacKenzie)

better than quote from the interesting letter he was good enough to send me, detailing some of the stories about Slaybrook. Brigadier Mackenzie tells me he has always been sceptical of ghost stories but having owned a number of old houses — including the oldest timbered frame mediaeval house in Kent, Eastling Manor, he has come to the conclusion that there are sometimes unexpected happenings in old houses. I found myself fully in agreement with him when he suggested that some old houses may absorb the crises, emotions and happiness of the families that lived in them, almost like a recording tape, and in their own way and time occasionally play back those scenes of past history.

'Previous owners have had mediums and other people round the house but whether their reports are genuine or not one cannot say. However there are four tales of ghostly happenings that may interest you:

Number 1 — The Slaybrook Battle. In Roman times the area of Slaybrook was a tribal settlement of Britons deep in the forests surrounding the Roman port of Lemanis (now Lympne). Through this forest ran the Roman road, Stone Street, to Canterbury. The Britons were in the habit of plundering the Roman supply wagons making their way from Lemanis to Canterbury. These raids got so bad that the Romans were forced to take punitive action by sending two legions of Roman soldiers to the settlement at Slaybrook. A very bloody battle ensued, finally ending in a massacre of all the Britons and their homes were burnt down. It is said that the brook ran with blood for a week; hence the name Slaybrook. The dying tribal chief laid a curse on the Romans for this massacre and foretold that future generations would be reminded of this ghastly deed.

Every year, between the months of December and January, strange flickering lights appear around the trees and gardens of Slaybrook. At first my wife and I thought it was lightning, but there were no sounds of a thunderstorm or lightning that accompanies it. Could this have been the message from the tribal chief reminding us of the great massacre? Past owners of Slaybrook Hall have seen, for a fleeting moment, the appearance of Roman soldiers in the brook.

Number 2 — The Five Knights. At the time of the murder of Thomas Becket, Archbishop of Canterbury, in 1170, Slaybrook was a hostelry less than a mile from Saltwood Castle. When nobles, bishops and other dignitaries stayed at the castle, it was usual for their retainers, and the grooms and their horses, to be lodged at Slaybrook where, often enough, fresh horses could be procured. The men preferred the relaxed atmosphere of the hostelry than to be subject to the restrictions and strict discipline of the castle garrison. In any case the merry and buxom Saltwood wenches serving at the hostelry were an added attraction and could be relied upon to give good value for money ... perhaps they are some of the happy ghosts of Slaybrook.

The murder of Thomas Becket is well known and recorded. The five knights involved were Randolph de Broc, Robert Fitzurse, Hugh de Moreville, William de Tracy and Richard de Bret and they plotted the murder in Saltwood Castle. Local legend now has it that after the murder the knights were warned not to return to the castle but to spend the night at the hostelry before leaving the district the next day.

An unusual incident happened when my family moved into Slaybrook. The next morning it was noticed that what appeared to be drops of blood were visible on our Elizabethan dining-table, marks that were very difficult to erase. Naturally I was annoyed and my first thought was that the roofing contractors had not done their job properly and so let the rain seep down the old timbers. However, this possibility was thoroughly checked and the roof was proved to be completely watertight. One can only surmise that perhaps the knights did dine in that room after the murder.

Number 3 — The Grey Lady. The 'Grey Lady' visitations have been reported many times. She seems to be seen only in the area of the small courtyard between the house and the brook. One afternoon I was mowing my front lawn and had just stopped to adjust the cutting blades of the mower when my attention was drawn to the figure of a woman who was bending over my rhododendron plants at about fifteen yards away adjacent to the courtyard. She was dressed in a long blue and white striped dress with a high ruff collar round the neck. Then like a flash she disappeared. Frankly I was astonished. I queried the dress of the Grey Lady and my wife pointed out that blue and white colours at a distance could well merge into the colour of grey. No one knows the story of the Grey Lady.

Perhaps she was one of the many owners who loved her house and especially the walk round the courtyard beside the brook.

Number 4 — The Incident in the Study. My painter and decorator, who is not usually perturbed by anything, was badly startled while working in my study. The door on his left opened and then he was thrust against the wall by an ice-cold presence which then immediately left by the door leading into our kitchen. My decorator told me that he would not work in that room alone with no one in the house. No explanation has ever been found for this curious incident.'

I am most grateful to Brigadier J.A. Mackenzie for such a lucid and interesting account of some of the puzzling happenings that have occurred at Slaybrook Hall. I am delighted to hear that Slaybrook Hall has been awarded a plaque by the Kent Historic Buildings Committee and can now be officially described as a Historic Building of Kent. It must be a place full of memories and associations from the past for Sir Gerald du Maurier was among previous owners and Sir Noel Coward was a frequent visitor and his plays were sometimes read in the forty-three foot drawing-room. 'Slaybrook Hall has a reputation for being the most haunted house in the area', Brigadier Mackenzie tells me, 'but that is an exaggeration. All I can say is that Slaybrook Hall is a happy place to own and live in, ghosts and all'.

Within the last few years mysterious lights and a strange and unexplained figure have been reported in the densely wooded area around Saltwood. Four teenagers, walking from Saltwood to Sandling, saw a ball of fire on the top of a hill about eighty feet away. Walking down a dip, they lost sight of it but when they continued up the opposite hill, a figure suddenly appeared on the road ahead, 'like a man in a red cloak carrying a lantern', one of them said. It shuffled up the hill and when it reached the railway bridge, disappeared. As they went down to the station they had to be careful not to slip on the frozen puddles, yet just outside the station, where the figure had vanished, it seemed quite warm.

A young man and his girl-friend were passing the football field at Brockhill School when they saw a strange light, a kind of glow, coming from behind some trees and lighting up the field. They could see a dark figure standing in the middle of the field. The light seemed brighter as they approached it and then, abruptly, it disappeared. The girl screamed and fainted.

There are a number of reports of a ghost being seen near Slaybrook Corner; some people think it is the ghost of William Tournay, a wealthy and eccentric landowner who died some seventy-five years ago and who is buried on an island in the middle of a nearby lake, but why his ghost should walk is not known.

## Sevenoaks

A seventeenth century coach-house here was once the home of singer Vince Hill and his wife Anne. They loved the oak beams, the sloping ceiling and the inglenook fireplace, but they only stayed for two years, for they discovered that they had moved in with a ghost!

'Our bedroom had horsebox doors and metal latches,' Vince Hill said afterwards. 'We often heard the most terrifying thud, thud, thud, going up the stairs — and there was never anything there . . . it happened three times when Anne was alone in the house . . . and we looked for another home . . . '

Fairlawne, drawn by George Shepherd c.1830

## Shipbourne

On the borders of Shipbourne and Plaxtol stands a house called Fairlawne, the largest and most important of the older properties in the area where there are several buildings dating from the fourteenth century.

Originally named Fairlayne because of its proximity to the highway leading to the Fair at Shipbourne, the history of the estate certainly goes back to the 1300s, according to the 1981 publication of Tonbridge and Malling District Council: *Plaxtol and Fairlawne: a Conservation Study*.

It is stated that from at least 1327 the Colpepper family possessed the estate until 1413, when it passed to the Chowe family who continued to live there for over two hundred years, until 1630 when it came into the ownership of Sir Henry Vane the Elder, Comptroller of the Royal Household of Henry VIII and later Secretary of State to Charles I.

Sir Henry's son, known as 'the younger', was undoubtedly instrumental in the impeachment of 'that great man' Thomas Wentworth, Earl of Strafford, who was executed on Tower Hill. In June, 1662, Vane had to answer the charge of high treason and, although he made a bold and skilful defence, he was found guilty and executed on Tower Hill twelve days later. It is his ghost that is said to walk at Fairlawne.

S.P.B. Mais has written of the ghost of Sir Henry Vane 'haunting the yews of Fairlawne' and it seems to have been common knowledge that at one time his ghost (with his head under his arm!), and also the ghost of his wife, haunted the Wilderness Walk in Fairlawne Park on the anniversary of the execution of Sir Henry. The Vane family remained at Fairlawne until 1789 and today 'Fairlawn' is a large house and estate.

## Sittingbourne

A Georgian, bow-fronted property here, once a dental surgery and later a small hotel and restaurant, has been reported to be haunted by the ghost of an unidentified man and possibly an unidentified woman too.

Several guests claimed to have encountered the ghost of a tall man in one particular bedroom early in the morning and, although the appearance does not appear to have been frightening in any way, the sound accompanying the apparition, a noise resembling very heavy breathing, is, say those who have heard it, more than slightly disturbing.

One day a young maid who had been working in the basement suddenly appeared upstairs and said she had been frightened by the ghostly form of a woman she had seen in the room where she had been working. The proprietor tended to dismiss the story and put it all down to an excuse for the girl to get out of the job she was supposed to be doing at the time; in any case the fact is that the girl went home and did not return.

In the High Street there is a haunted building that started life as a brewery, later becoming a theatre and, inevitably, perhaps these days, later still, a bingo hall.

When it was a brewery, perhaps a century ago, one Sunday evening a night worker fell into one of the huge vats and drowned. He was not missed, it seems, and was eventually only discovered the following day.

In the part of this building corresponding to the place where once the fatal accident happened, a shadowy figure has been reportedly seen by various people;

the temperature is said to drop dramatically on occasions and various odd sounds and experiences are attributed to the ghostly activity of the man who drowned in stewing malt. What is interesting is that all the reports occur on Sunday nights.

## Sissinghurst

Here once stood the house and home of Sir Richard 'Bloody' Baker, otherwise known as the English Bluebeard. Chancellor to Mary Tudor 'that sallow-faced zealot whose passion and religion combined to warp her judgment' (as Richard Church put it) he imprisoned and tortured Protestants in the odd little apartment over the south porch of the parish church, known as Baker's Hole, before burning them at the stake.

A monster of a man who made a fortune out of plundering and murdering his neighbours and friends and acquaintances in the name of religion, he built himself a showy palace which Horace Walpole described on a visit in 1752; ending by saying: 'The whole is built for show; for the back of the house is nothing but lath and plaster . . . ' Three thousand French prisoners of the Napoleonic Wars hastened the decay of the place which came, in time, a poorhouse. It was left to Sir Harold and Lady Nicolson to bring a new glory to Sissinghurst but before we leave the old house there is a tale to tell.

The story goes that the girl he was betrothed to took a girl friend on a surprise visit to meet Sir Richard, ignoring a squawking parrot who gave them warning: "Peapot, pretty lady, be not bold; Or your red blood will soon run cold."

Hearing Sir Richard approaching, they hid beneath the stairs, thinking to surprise him. They were themselves surprised to see him enter and climb the stairs carrying the corpse of his latest victim, and when its stiffened hand caught in the bannisters, Sir Richard simply hacked it off — and it fell into the lap of one of the young ladies crouching there in hiding! By means of a ring on one of the fingers the victim was identified, Sir Richard was brought to justice at last . . . and his ghost was long said to frequent the place.

Another ghost at Sissinghurst is that of a priest who has been seen and heard both in the garden and in the vicinity of the old castle. In the 1950s Felix Seward, Chairman of the Ghost Club from 1954 to 1960, knew both Sir Harold and Lady Nicolson and, knowing of his great interest in psychic matters, they talked freely to him about the ghost priest, thought to have been walled-up alive, the mysterious and unaccountable footsteps and other apparently paranormal activity in the beautiful place they had created at Sissinghurst.

Walking in this enchanting garden today it seems impossible to believe that when the Nicolsons came it was a wilderness without a path or a plant, for today the long axial walks, the enclosures — each at its best at a different season; the lovely old roses, the herb garden, thyme lawn and stone paths are everything an old and seasoned garden should be; a magic place and an ideal setting for a gentle ghost.

Sissinghurst Castle in 1760

I once had lunch with Sir Harold at his London club and I found this seasoned diplomat, respected biographer and acknowledged critic no disbeliever in psychic happenings; indeed he told me that he had had experiences that had utterly convinced him of the possibility of such occurrences and he reminded me, with that shrewd glance of his, that the title of one of his books was: *Another World Than This*.

Sir Harold had no qualms in telling me about the ghost priest that haunted the gardens he and his wife had created and he told me how excited they had been when they had come across the story about a priest being walled-up at Sissinghurst. Sir Harold said his wife felt that perhaps the restful and timeless quality that the gardens had acquired may have tempted the unquiet spirit of the sad priest to seek some peace there and they both felt happy about that.

Other evidence for the ghostly figure has come from reliable Mrs Hayter, Sir Harold's trusted housekeeper, and from many visitors who have made enquiries about the identity of the 'reverend gentleman' they had seen walking alone and, it seemed, making no sound as he passed. Other visitors reported hearing the sound of footsteps beside them as they enjoyed the quiet and beauty of the gardens, soft and shuffling, like sandals, but they have seen nothing that could have accounted for the sounds.

Interestingly enough Sir Harold had the occasional habit of clicking his teeth with his tongue, a peculiarity that was well-known among his sophisticated young gentlemen friends and after his death 'a mysterious clicking noise' was repeatedly reported in various parts of the property, usually by young men; among them Peter South who was living on the estate at the time.

There is a tranquil air of mystery and enchantment at Sissinghurst and it seems likely that the Nicolsons, unknowingly and unconsciously, have left behind something of their great love for the place and provided the environment for psychic activity.

I first heard of the haunting of a house called Branden from my good friend Air Commodore R. Carter Jonas OBE of Fowey. Some fifty years ago he visited the house in the Weald with an acquaintance of Ian Davison, at that time the owner and occupier of the property. Davison was a former stage actor and friend of Scouts and ex-prisoners; a lover of nature and naturism. He had purchased Branden in the early 1930s and subsequently wrote about the house and its ghosts in *Where Smugglers Walked* (1935).

Carter Jonas has always been interested in ghosts and haunted houses and in fact he invented a fascinating and unique filing and reference system on ghosts which he has recently been kind enough to pass over to me. He asked Davison about any ghosts at Branden and then learned firsthand the story of the various ghosts and ghostly happenings — and in particular about a rather frightening phantom named Tarver. Subsequently Ian Davison wrote his book and recounted virtually exactly what he had told Carter Jonas. As soon as I heard about the hauntings I contacted the present owner, Nigel E.M. Gunnis, who bought the house from Ian Davison and has lived there for over thirty years.

During all his busy acting years in London and the provinces Davison always longed for a house in the country and he never forgot the words of his old nurse when he was very young: 'his life shall be surrounded with flowers' she had said, but after leaving Harrow he immediately went on the stage and for some ten years toured in revues or played in London productions . . . then he found Branden. When he bought the place there were rickety cow sheds roofed with corrugated iron, a once-magnificent barn in a sorry plight, an uninhabited house half-buried by rubbish and brambles but with a lovely long deep roof of mellowed tiles; an old-world baking oven and iron-latticed windows; heaps of rusted iron almost hid an oast-house and the remains of pig-sties, and nearby a deep moat was filled with stagnant water.

From his very first day at Branden Ian Davison maintained that a number of strange happenings occurred. Almost every night he would be awakened by the sound of footsteps inside or possibly outside the house. At first he thought a tramp may have been using the house or barn and was paying nocturnal visits, but then he noticed that his dog, 'a tiger-marked Great Dane' who never showed fear of any human being, seemed to be very frightened at the sound of the footsteps and would not accompany his master when Davison set out to search for the cause of the mysterious sounds. There were quick, sharp raps at one of the windows too, as though someone was knocking on the pane . . . Davison called out, asking who was there and when there was no reply he made his way to the

Branden near Sissinghurst

window which was open and called again; there was still no answer and no explanation but Peter heard the knockings and would growl ominously. And there was an even more puzzling occurrence. A large room on the ground floor was being restored so Ian and his friend Euan used the smaller, square room with one window and two doors; neither liked the room and although it was by now April the room always seemed to be icy cold, despite the fire that burned all day; and then sometimes, for no apparent reason, the room would suddenly become unbearably hot and seem devoid of all air. A strong musty smell would float through the room on occasions and in the mornings, on first entering the room, there was a strange, clammy atmosphere about it.

Soon Ian found that he was unable to stay long in this room without feeling dizzy and he noticed that Euan, after sitting in the room for a while, would fall asleep and then drop into a kind of stupor. One night Euan, having fallen into the drowsy, stupor-like sleep, suddenly started up with a gasp, raising his hands to his throat . . . He said he must have been dreaming but he had the distinct impression that someone had come up behind him and seized him by the throat. Ian Davison was so interested that he resolved the next time he felt dizzy in the room he would not leave but remain in the room and see what would transpire.

It happened the following night: first the room grew very hot and airless; Ian got up and opened the window as far as possible but it made not the slightest difference; he walked about the room which had become almost unbearably oppressive. Euan was looking pale and drowsy. By now Ian was feeling very dizzy and finding it difficult to breathe; he staggered to the door, a mist thickening across his eyes, but he managed to reach the outer door and then collapsed. When he came round he felt perfectly well and he returned to the room. There was now no one but himself in the room but again he noticed a putrid, heavy smell and having had enough for one night he prepared to go to bed. Meeting Euan, also preparing to retire, he learned that the room was affecting him in much the same way. 'There's something ghastly about that room . . . it's horrible', Euan said and then he revealed that twice he had had the impression that someone had grabbed him round the throat. The following day Ian and Euan had a friend Mervyn staying with them and they were surprised to find him in bed in daytime. He said he had been writing letters in the little square room and had suddenly fainted — something he had never done before in his life — and he thought he had better go to bed.

One night Ian Davison was awakened by the sound of footsteps and although he had become accustomed to them by this time he had still not discovered their origin and this particular night, for some reason, he felt he had a good chance of discovering the explanation for alterations had resulted in an empty window space in the big room and it was from there that the sound of footsteps seemed to originate: heavy, tramping sounds. Davison jumped out of bed, causing the old floorboards to creak, and the footsteps ceased abruptly. Davison stood very still and listened for he knew he would hear any sound in the room below, and soon the mysterious visitor recommenced his perambulations. Davison listened for several minutes; the sounds suggested someone wandering about the room as though in search of something. Eventually they came to a standstill beside the fireplace, where Davison and his friends had removed hundreds of bricks to reveal a glorious open hearth, twelve feet long and four feet deep. Davison stood stock still and listened but there was no further movement and very quietly he moved to the window. Dawn was almost breaking and he sat on the window-sill and waited for daylight. This time he felt sure he would catch his nocturnal visitor for the clutter and rubble that lay about the big room would prevent anyone from moving and certainly from leaving without making quite a noise. As dawn broke Davison could contain himself no longer and carefully and quietly he moved across the window-ledge, caught the sill and lowered himself over, dropping on to the soft earth below; then he looked into the big room — it was empty. There was not a trace of a boot or shoe or any sign of anything being disturbed; yet he had heard heavy, tramping footsteps from this room.

During the three years that he spent at Branden before writing his book Ian Davison heard similar heavy footsteps many, many times and once he was awakened by Peter to hear something else. He was awakened by the dog growling and at first he thought everything was quiet but then he heard what the dog must have heard long before him. The sound of approaching footsteps came through the open windows, seemingly from somewhere near the oast-house; they were not heavy or very distinct, but definite, hurrying footsteps. Were these the footsteps that so frequently disturbed him at night, Davison wondered . . . then he heard a door creak and he sat up in bed. Then more footsteps, now very distinct; then a clattering noise that made Peter whine with fear. Distinct footsteps rang upon the stone paving outside and Davison thought he could distinguish the sounds of two men running. They seemed to pass below his window and run round the corner of the house which meant they would pass beneath the other window of his room. He jumped out of bed and raced to the window but it was too dark to see anything, but as he leaned out of the window he could still hear the footsteps. When they reached the north end of the house, there was a terrific crash, which seemed to make the whole house shake. Davison lit a candle (for electricity had not then been installed) and hurried into the passage where he met his servant who commented: 'The chimney must have fallen down . . . ' The large kitchen chimney was being repaired at the time so this seemed a reasonable conclusion. Together the two men went downstairs, found a storm lantern, and went outside. The chimney had not fallen down. They searched all round the house but could find no sign of anything having been disturbed. In the morning they inspected the whole place again. Nothing was out of place and there was no logical explanation for the loud crashing noise — or for the running footsteps.

Davison came to the conclusion that what he had heard was some kind of echo from the past — perhaps a smuggler being chased, possibly the discharge of a musket at the corner of the house during a hand-to-hand fight . . . Ridiculous as all this may sound Davison told himself that Marconi believed that no sound was ever lost but continued in the ether surrounding the world . . . if all sounds do somehow remain, may it not be possible that at certain times waves vibrate and cause the place whence the sounds originated to act as a receiver and again record the sound? Soon however Ian Davison was to experience stranger things than sounds.

Davison states in his book that he had never felt or known the terror that many people have of ghosts. He considered it as natural that there might be a shadowy world of beings 'we cannot know, or easily see or touch or feel' and although he did not profess any great knowledge or experience of the subject, his long interest and study of nature, he felt, had taught him to believe that there exists more on this earth than can be accounted for; and this belief resulted in the complete absence of fear in respect of things that frighten many people. Once, in London, he saw the ghost of a man in the house where he had a flat and where he experienced almost nightly such occurrences as door-opening, a current of wind, footsteps, bell-ringing and knocks.

Eventually hardly a day passed without Davison experiencing something odd and apparently inexplicable at Branden: curious noises, loud crashes, an unpleasant atmosphere in the square room which he came to regard as useless except as a box room, for no one would sleep in it for more than one night; unnatural coldness; excessive heat; strange 'shadows' that vanished mysteriously; unaccountable currents of air; once he found the clear imprint of a claw-like hand in dust upon a table in the early morning; visitors recounted strange and worrying dreams and hurriedly cut short their visits and left the house. Stories of the odd happenings spread about the neighbourhood and one man, a sceptic who was much amused at the stories, sometimes stayed at Branden and he turned out to be the first person to see a phantom form inside the house. He and his wife were sleeping in Davison's room and he was above them in the attic. In the adjoining room there was another visitor, a lady. The morning after their arrival the couple asked Davison about the rumpus in the night — but Davison had heard nothing. 'I'm not laughing at ghosts any more', his friend added. 'I saw one last night'. Apparently he had found himself suddenly wide awake in the middle of the night and he had seen a small woman 'come through the door that leads into your lady visitor's room; she was carrying a tumbler in her hand and at first I thought it was your visitor . . . I asked her what she wanted but she didn't answer and then I realised it wasn't who I thought it was, though she was about the same height. I spoke to her again but she still didn't answer and continued walking very slowly towards me. I sat up in bed and looked at her . . . she gave me the creeps. My shoes were by the bed so I picked one up and threw it at her but missed her; I snatched up the other one, threw it, and it went clean through her! Then she slowly walked away and disappeared into the wall!' His wife had been disturbed by the noise of his shoes being thrown across the room and found him sitting up in bed, petrified with fright. 'Could he have been dreaming?' Davison asked her. 'Oh no,' she replied. 'He was very much awake — in fact, he was half out of bed!' She had not seen the figure but was very conscious of a heavy and oppressive atmosphere in the room which remained for a long time.

A few days later Davison saw the same little woman himself and later he came to know her well by sight for he saw her many times. She was always dressed in grey and wore a shawl over her shoulders. She had a very sad expression and looked rather 'simple', not quite half-witted but slightly stupid and lacking in intelligence. It was about four o'clock one afternoon when he first saw her. She appeared to be wandering aimlessly around the fireplace in his bedroom — the room in which she had been seen previously. She was slightly bent and her eyes seemed to be searching the ground as though she was looking for something. There was nothing about the figure that was at all frightening to Davison; on the contrary she roused in him a great sense of pity: she seemed so cowed and miserable, a forlorn little thing — and he wished he could comfort her but his presence seemed to frighten her and, soon after he had entered the room, she disappeared into the wall.

Following the first appearance of the little old woman manifestations seemed to become even more frequent and for the first time Davison noticed a strange phenomenon which he was at a complete loss to understand: whenever anything very odd was about to happen he would have a warning in the form of a large shadow, resembling the form of a man, that would come out of the wall of the big room downstairs, float into the centre of the room, then turn and pass back into the large open fireplace where it would vanish. This form was always very dim and shadowy and would be visible only a short time but during the period the shadow was present the room would become very cold. The dogs that Davison had at this time hated this manifestation and would follow the course that the shadow took with frightened eyes. Often the shadow would appear between seven and nine in the evening and whenever it did appear something very strange would take place later that night. The shadowy form was seen one February evening when Davison had staying with him a lady who was nervous about such things and a man named Drew who had a dog, which slept in the big room.

Davison woke suddenly that night in the early hours to find his friend's dog scratching on his bedroom door and whining nervously. Davison jumped out of bed and found, to his amazement, that he was drenched with perspiration. He opened the door and let the dog into the room, then he lit a lamp. He found the atmosphere in the room quite extraordinary; like warm vapour, almost comparable to the hot room of a Turkish bath. Peter, his own dog, was panting on his bed and whining in a frightened way; the other dog climbed on to Davison's bed and lay there trembling. The heat was tremendous and for a moment Davison thought the house must be on fire . . . he tore off his wet pyjamas and crossed to the window, which was open, and stood there naked. Outside it was snowing softly, yet the room was so hot that it was practically unbearable! Suddenly his attention was drawn to his bedroom door. Very slowly it was becoming transparent, from right to left — just as though it was being pushed slowly into the wall. He gazed in astonishment and, as the door completely vanished, leaving an opening where it had been, he saw standing in the passage, 'the foulest-looking man' he had ever set eyes on. Well over six feet in height, thickly built and dressed in a gaudy medley of brightly-coloured clothes: Davison could not hazard a guess as to the period to which they belonged but they were certainly tawdry and old, although not by any means ragged. The man had a large body 'of fine proportions' but his face was revolting: the cheeks were broad and tanned, the jaw thick, the eyes and hair dark, and the mouth ugly in the extreme: the thick red lips parted in a devilish grin to reveal two rows of enormous yellow teeth.

The figure stood quite still, leering. As Davison tried to address the awesome form the grin seemed to become broader still until the whole face seemed to be nothing but mouth . . . and then a fiendish peal of laughter filled the air. Davison looked away from the revolting face and when he looked back the door was slowly closing over the terrifying figure, moving this time from left to right, and a moment later there was nothing to be seen. The dogs were shivering with fright and Davison discovered that it was four o'clock in the morning. Much later, when his servant called him, he said: 'What a terrible heat-wave swept through the house last night!' 'At what time —' Davison asked. 'About four,' came the answer. 'It was awful — I could hardly breathe.' Later still that morning his lady guest reported that she had heard loud and persistent noises issuing from the room below hers (she was above the room that often had a strange atmosphere) and she thought a fight of some sort was taking place; she had lit a light and remained sitting on the bed shivering with fright for the rest of the night; and she returned to London the next day. His guest Drew, on the other hand, had slept undisturbed throughout the night, the only person in the house to do so, although he did complain of being very tired in the morning. Davison said it was a curious fact that at this period whenever a manifestation took place, one person in the house would always be in a very deep sleep.

One night Davison and a friend he had staying with him, Bill, took the dogs out for a run. Bill was open-minded on the subject of ghosts, perhaps inclined to be a little sceptical but he suddenly wished to take part in a ghost-hunt. Davison told him there was no point in looking for them, they did not appear to have any special 'haunts'; they just appeared at odd times anywhere in the house. This information only encouraged Bill to suggest that perhaps they would see one that night; but Davison was not optimistic for he had seen no shadow in the big room that evening and he had come to place great faith in that warning. They were returning from their walk when suddenly the dogs, about two yards ahead of Davison and his friend, came to a sudden halt simultaneously and stood, rigid, their hackles rising, their ears forward, their muzzles pointing towards the upper part of the house which they watched intently. Davison and Bill followed their gaze but could see nothing. Suddenly a low moaning sound came from the house; it rose in volume until it reached a 'crescendo of agony' and then gradually faded away. Davison described it as an eerie sound, 'intense with pain' that sent a cold shiver down the watchers' backs.

As time went by more and more people suggested to Davison that he should do something about the ghosts but he felt he knew they were there, he accepted them as something he did not understand and could not control and there he let the matter rest; until one day Denis Conan Doyle called to show Davison a new racing car he had bought. Davison told him about the mysterious happenings and Denis Conan Doyle told him that the heat-wave suggested that the haunts were evil and he said he knew someone who might be able to help: Ronald Kaulback, an explorer and experienced psychic investigator.

The following afternoon Denis Conan Doyle visited Branden again, bringing with him his brother Adrian and Ronald Kaulback. Kaulback immediately felt 'the most intense fear' he had ever known in the room with the strange atmosphere and shortly afterwards he fell into a deep sleep in the haunted room, beside the fireplace, breathing in the most extraordinary way and gasping for breath. Davison and Denis Conan Doyle thought they saw a 'shadow' creeping round Ronald's neck and they found that an invisible force was apparently trying to strangle Ronald; when Adrian came into the room he added his weight against the invisible but seemingly very solid force and eventually they broke it and it disappeared. When Ronald came round he was quite unaware of anything that had happened but Davison and the Conan Doyle brothers were utterly convinced that he had been very near to being strangled.

The following morning Denis and Adrian Conan Doyle had to leave but Ronald stayed for some weeks with Davison at Branden and the ghosts became 'very active and appeared in far more definite shape than they had previously done'. There now appeared to be at least three ghosts: the little old woman in grey; the foul and fearsome male figure and another man who was short and thickly built and very ugly but his appearance never caused Davison any feelings of repulsion. Then there was the phantom cat, which often seemed to be about at this time, a small black furry form that jumped out of the wall and ran all over the house causing a lot of panic for it was quite impossible to touch it. It made an odd sort of noise which Davison described as 'a mixture of purring and flapping wings'. The strange shadowy form continued to appear in the big room, often about seven o'clock in the evening when anything unusual was likely to occur later that night. Ronald and Davison saw it simultaneously several times and to eliminate the possibility of their being influenced by imagination, they arranged not to mention anything either of them saw until it had passed. Invariably they found that they had both seen the shadow at the same time.

Several mediums visited the house at this time and one, who said she had visited similar haunted houses in France, believed that Branden was haunted by the evil spirits of people who had once practiced black magic there. Much of what she said, Davison, felt, made sense of many of the mysterious happenings at Branden: the foul-smelling moat; circles, squares and triangles that formed parts of the house; its squareness, facing towards the four points of the compass; magic circles guarding the entrances — circles that were often made with the help of sacrificed babies and when they lifted the floor at one spot indicated by the medium, they found fragments of very small bones, 'that could only have been those of a baby' says Davison. (Years later Davison told Nigel Gunnis that they could have been chicken bones — but who on earth would bury chicken bones underneath floorboards?)

With the help of information that he obtained from several mediums Davison believed that he discovered some of the dark history of Branden. He thought that a group of black magic devotees had lived there and in particular one satanist named George Tarver who inherited the isolated house and found it ideal for his orgies. Tarver had formed a coven, practised every form of demonology and necromancy and in time Branden came to be shunned by local people who whispered about women who disappeared and human sacrifices... Among Tarver's followers was a man named Hunter who was not evil by nature but who came under Tarver's power. A woman whose baby had been slaughtered as a sacrifice was sent mad and all day she would roam the house in search of her child. She had been Tarver's mistress but one day, in a fit of rage, he murdered her — in the smaller room, downstairs. Hunter witnessed the murder and Tarver killed him too and buried his body in the grounds: this murder of a member of the coven roused the remainder of the circle to action and eventually Tarver was hanged from a beam in the big room.

Then, for some years, Branden was empty. At one time it was occupied by descendants of the Flemish weavers who came to England in the fourteenth century. Cranbrook, only three miles away, was at that time the capital of the Weald and Branden was eminently suitable for a fulling mill as a stream ran past the house. A raised bank, some eight feet high, stretched across the orchard and was once the mill dam; a path nearby was known as Smugglers' Walk and is part of the accepted Smugglers' Walk that used to run from Sissinghurst to the sea and there is little doubt that at one time Branden did know smugglers.

Some months after Ronald Kaulback had left Branden to explore Tibet and write *Tibetan Trek*, Davison was alone in the house when the strangest of all the manifestations at Branden took place. One evening, after tea, he went upstairs on his way to the bathroom and although he and others saw manifestations at Branden at all hours of the day and night, he was not thinking about ghosts or expecting to see one at that time when he suddenly encountered Tarver standing in front of the bathroom door. He was only three feet away, a massive figure, smiling triumphantly, the very emblem of strength and power. A sudden terror seized Davison and he turned and ran down the stairs — and then he stopped and turned back and faced Tarver, who was still only a few feet away; but Davison felt that he must exert his ownership of the house once and for all. He took a step forward. 'You must get out of my way', he said, although he knew that his voice quavered. Tarver did not move. Davison returned his gaze and endeavoured to concentrate every ounce of strength and determination on opposing the force he was facing. In a matter of seconds — although it seemed much longer — Tarver slowly moved across the passage. 'This house is mine', shouted Davison. 'My will is stronger than yours . . . your presence is not wanted here . . . you must go . . . it does not matter what holds you here . . . Go! and go now! . . . ' Slowly the form dissolved, became transparent, vague and finally faded into the wall. Davison felt sick with fear but he also felt that he was now free of Tarver and although he did see the same form later, it was only in very shadowy and vague form.

Davison felt that his mental battle with the phantom form of Tarver in some way affected the other ghosts that had haunted Branden. One afternoon he was brushing his hair in front of the dressing-table in a corner of his bedroom when some instinct told him to turn round and when he did so he saw the little old woman beside the fireplace, the place where she usually appreared. Previously she had always seemed to be searching for something but this time she seemed to look straight at Davison; she seemed changed in other ways too, she looked different somehow and a smile played around her lips. The sadness seemed to have gone; she looked younger and happier. Slowly she raised her arms and held them stretched out towards Davison, as though saying farewell. She smiled and slowly passed back into the wall and was never seen again.

A few nights later Davison was lying awake in bed; it was a clear, bright night and he could plainly see every part of the bedroom. Suddenly he was aware that the man he knew as Hunter was standing beside his bed. He looked sadder than usual and, as always in the presence of this form, Davison felt quite unafraid and he asked whether he could help Hunter in any way. The form did not answer but bent over him until it almost touched Davison's face and the eyes gazed into his, beseechingly it seemed. Davison told Hunter to stay beside him if he could comfort him, for he had become accustomed to speaking to his ghosts in exactly the same way that he would speak to ordinary people; Hunter looked so tired that Davison invited him to lie down on the bed, but the form continued to look at him with sad eyes, still leaning over him, and so it remained for what seemed a long time. Davison did not know what to do. He wondered whether he should try to touch the figure but he did not do so. After about twenty minutes the form quietly departed.

The following day a friend who was interested in spiritualism came to stay at Branden and during the first night, which she spent in a room adjoining Davison's, directly above the room with the strange atmosphere, she had a curious experience. She awakened suddenly in the middle of the night to find the bedclothes in a heap at the bottom of the bed and when she leaned forward to pull them back she noticed that the room seemed to be growing lighter, due to a sort of mist that appeared to be rising upwards from the bedroom floor. Then, from the far right-hand side of the room, the figure of a man appeared and walked slowly towards the bed. When he reached the side of the bed the occupant wanted to scream but something impelled her to look straight at the man and when she did so she became aware that he was not evil and she felt that he was trying to get away from something or break free in some way. She described the figure she saw as shortish, with broad shoulders, and wearing an old and shabby swallow-tail coat. He had long arms and almost dead-white hands; a square head and deep-set forehead; large and rather protruding green-blue eyes, a long thin nose, sunken cheeks and bright red lips. Then she seemed to see a signpost and something told her to ask the form which way he wanted to go. She seemed to think that he replied, 'the right way' and stretched out a hand which she took and held for a long time in a firm grip. Then, in the distance as it were, she heard a faint purring sound combined with a flapping noise which came nearer and nearer. The man at her bedside turned and looked in the direction from which the noise came, then quickly turned and vanished at about the spot where she had first seen him. The visitor waited, wide awake, in the room that was still lit by a strange light. After a while she felt a strangling sensation which soon ceased and the room became dark and she fell asleep. The ghost called Hunter was never seen again.

A few shadowy forms continued to appear at Branden, according to Ian Davison, but gradually they became less distinct and eventually they ceased altogether. The black cat ceased to appear with the departure of Tarver and Davison thought these two ghostly forms were affiliated in some way for he had noticed that often an appearance of the cat would be succeeded by one of Tarver. The strange noises gradually ceased too and after a few months the queer happenings at Branden all ceased completely. Davison said at the time: 'Why or how they came to an end I do not know. Possibly some of the people who came to exorcise the ghosts achieved success; or it may have been that with the change of air currents the house no longer acted as a receiver to the wave-lengths that vibrated these things. Neither do I know that they have departed for ever — it may all happen again.' Yet the ghosts at Branden do seem to have been laid or become quiescent for in 1982 Nigel Gunnis told me: 'We have been here over thirty years and have yet to see a ghost or experience any manifestation — but you never know!'

In May 1984 charming Diana and Nigel Gunnis showed my wife and me over their beautiful home; the original parts of the house that may go back as far as the fourteenth century, the later additions and alterations made by Ian Davison (who died a couple of years before my visit to Branden) and the still later alterations and additions by Mr and Mrs Gunnis that have made a gloomy house that was full of shadows into a really lovely home.

Diana and Nigel Gunnis are cousins and their mutual grandmother was the wife of Colonel Streatfeild of Chiddingstone Castle and the sister of Lady Strathmore who married the 13th Earl of Glamis Castle, possibly the most haunted castle in the world.

To me there is still an atmosphere in the so-called 'big room' and in the room that Ian Davison said he and many other people felt violent and inexplicable changes of heat and cold and where, it would seem, ghosts once walked. Now there are only vague stories of a dark figure glimpsed in the garden. A former gardener named Luck, who worked at Branden from the time Nigel Gunnis bought the place until he died, said he once saw someone go into the barn and went to investigate but found no one. Nigel Gunnis tells me that Luck was a very down to earth countryman and was completely convinced that he had seen someone enter the barn. Sometime in the last century a man hanged himself in the barn.

Today the garden at Branden is a perfect joy and as I sat and talked with Nigel Gunnis the years seemed to fall away and I almost thought I saw Branden as it had been fifty years ago when, according to Ian Davison and others, the house was haunted and mysterious happenings occurred with alarming frequency at this beautiful, secluded and now peaceful spot.

## Smarden

The fourteenth century Chequers Inn has long been reputedly haunted by 'the ghost of a murdered man' but whether he was an English soldier, home from the Napoleonic Wars, or a French prisoner of war trying to escape from nearby Sissinghurst Castle, the story handed down is that he was murdered for the money that he carried. If the victim was an English soldier, it could have been for his pay which had mounted up while he was on active service; if an escaping prisoner, perhaps the money he had somehow acquired to make good his escape.

At all events there have been many reports of the sounds of someone impatiently pacing back and forth between two of the oldest bedrooms here and since The Chequers is said to have stood here for six centuries there must be many possible claimants for the doubtful honour of being the restless ghost. As with so many old Kent inns, it was once used by smugglers and it could well be that the ghost dates from that period.

The invisible presence has been known to upset dogs, notoriously supersensitive creatures, and it is said that one Afghan hound became so troubled by the inexplicable sounds that a vet had to be called to calm it.

## Southborough

Some years ago when the sixteenth century house known as Winton Lodge was occupied by Mr and Mrs H. Lloyd, they believed the property was haunted by the ghost of Queen Caroline, the unhappy wife of George IV, who is said to have stayed at the house, with her little daughter the Princess Charlottle, late in the eighteenth century when the area around Tunbridge Wells was favoured by the nobility. Perhaps the Queen enjoyed her stay in the quiet Kent countryside and, after death, returned to the place where she had, for a brief time, been happy.

At all events Mrs Lloyd told me that one afternoon, as she approached the side door of the house, she saw a lady standing there; 'a lady wearing an old-fashioned white dress, almost as though she were about to attend a fancy dress ball'. The figure seemed not to be aware of Mrs Lloyd's presence and so she addressed the motionless figure. 'Good afternoon,' she began — and then stopped short, for the mysterious lady in white had completely disappeared.

Mr and Mrs Lloyd moved into Winton Lodge in 1937 and over the years they experienced a wealth of strange happenings; by 1948 the local newspaper was referring to the place as 'surely the most haunted house in Southborough'. The reputation of the house for being haunted and that the ghost was that of Queen Caroline has been well known in the area for many years and although the Lloyds were not aware that the house was reputed to be haunted when they moved in, they never minded the odd occurrences and when Mr Lloyd was asked if it worried him that he lived in a haunted house, he replied, cheerfully, 'Not a scrap!'

One of the most frequently reported and totally unexplained happenings was the switching-on of the lights in the top storey of the house. This would happen time and time again when it was satisfactorily established that no human being could have touched the switches . . . Then there were the footsteps, strange, unhurried but oddly quiet footsteps that were heard in various parts of the house. One night both Mr and Mrs Lloyd heard footsteps pass their bedroom door, go downstairs and after a pause, come upstairs again. Each thought the other to be asleep and said nothing at the time but in the morning they discovered that they had both heard the footsteps. The only other person in the house at the time was their son Geoffrey who had not left his room.

On another occasion when they heard the footsteps go past their bedroom door and then down the stairs, Mr Lloyd quietly left his room and ascertained that Geoffrey was fast asleep. He then went downstairs to try to find the cause of the footsteps. He found nothing and after looking in each of the rooms downstairs, returned upstairs whereupon his wife told him that after he had gone downstairs and before he had returned, the footsteps had come back upstairs and past their bedroom door! It seemed that something invisible and inaudible must have passed Mr Lloyd; something whose footsteps only sounded on the stairway.

A bedstead in one of the bedrooms at Winton Lodge was shaken by some invisible presence in the middle of the night on several occasions; once a 'strange phenomenon' was reported by a visitor who knew nothing about any strange happenings in the house but she would never sleep in that room again.

A doorway at the side of the house, known as Queen Caroline's Door, seemed to exude a peculiar atmosphere and the Lloyds told me that their dog would never go near that particular door. Once or twice they tried to tempt him by placing his food in the doorway but he either made a wild grab at it and retreated to consume the food elsewhere or left the food alone and went without until it was placed elsewhere. This is the same doorway where the 'White Lady' was seen.

## Southfleet

The beautiful eleventh century house that used to be known as Southfleet Rectory was long reputed to be haunted. The ghosts include that of a woman whose body was said to have been bricked-up in the cellars; a monk who appeared most frequently in the appropriately named Monks Room; and a lady in a brown nun-like habit who may or may not be associated with the female who is supposed to have been immured in the cellar.

The first Rector of Southfleet was appointed in 1155 when Southfleet was an appanage of the See of Rochester; some eight hundred years later the incumbent was the Rev. W.M. Falloon and from him I heard details of the evidence for this interesting case of haunting. Subsequently I obtained verification from many sources.

There is no doubt that good evidence exists for ghostly appearances here for more than a century for, in the Monks Room, the room long regarded as the most haunted room in this fascinating house, there is a stained-glass window commemorating the fact that in 1874 the then Bishop of Rochester, the Rt Rev. P.L. Claughton, visited the rectory for the express purpose of performing a service of exorcism to lay the ghost.

During the incumbency of the Rev. J.H. Hazel, from 1891 to 1898, several appearances of a ghostly female were reported. On one occasion, three visitors apologised at breakfast on their first morning for coming to stay while there was

Southfleet Rectory. The Monks Room on the right is the oldest part of the house.

sickness in the house. They said they had all been visited by a nurse during the night. They were told there was no sick person in the house; there was no nurse in the house; and no mortal person had visited them during the night. Interestingly enough Mr Falloon, when he saw the ghost in 1942, noted several inches of white material showing at the cuffs of her sleeves, and this aspect, he felt, could well have accounted for the visitors regarding their nocturnal visitor as a nurse; although he was quite sure that the figure he saw was a nun. What would appear to have been the same figure was seen several times by members of the Hazel family and, later, by members of the Alcock family, as well as by visitors with no knowledge of the alleged ghost, during the sojourn of the Alcocks from 1908 to 1919.

Mrs Walcott Crockett, whose husband, the Rev. A.W. Crockett was Rector of Southfleet from 1920 to 1926, has given me details pertaining to the haunting of the rectory as she remembered them. She told me that her husband often talked happily of his days at Southfleet Rectory — although they both knew the place was haunted. Mrs Walcott Crockett's recollection of the origin of the ghost concerned a nurse who came to the rectory many years previously to care for a member of the family then in residence. The person who was ill died; there was some dispute about the possession of important family documents and thereafter the ghostly figure of a nurse seemed to have haunted the house.

As well as being seen — sometimes a complete materialisation, sometimes only partially visible and indistinct — footsteps of the ghost nurse have been heard walking swiftly and purposefully along a passage; the rustle of papers and of starched uniform have been heard; and a clicking noise, comparable to that made when locking or unlocking a door, was occasionally reported.

The Rev. B.S.W. Crockett, son of the late Rev. A.W. Crockett who died in 1950, has told me that he well recalls a servant at Southfleet Rectory seeing and describing in some detail the figure of a lady who held rustling papers in her hand and appeared to be searching for something or someone. He said that although the figure has been described as a nurse, he has always felt that she might be a nun for mediaeval portions of the rectory were formerly a monastic cell attached to Rochester Priory, and Mr Crockett suggested to me that the unhappy and unquiet lady may well be from a neighbouring convent.

Mrs Gertrude Dancy (née Burton) of Charmouth, Dorset, told me that while she was in the employ of the Rev. and Mrs Crockett at Southfleet Rectory between 1919 and 1920, she saw the ghost on one occasion. It was about 7.30 p.m. and she had occasion to go up to the housekeeper's room to prepare the bed for the night. This room was situated in the front part of the house. While working on the bed, Gertrude heard a sound like paper being dragged along the passage and she went to the bedroom door to see what was happening. Nothing was visible however, and the noise ceased as soon as she reached the door.

Returning to her task of making the housekeeper's bed, Gertrude then heard a louder noise, which she likened to the sound of a rustling skirt. Again it seemed to come from outside the room and again she went into the passage, carrying with her a small lighted lamp. Mrs Dancy's report continues:

'I stood at the top of a small stair just outside the room and to my surprise I saw a nurse dressed in a clean staff uniform standing at the end of the passage. She looked quite normal and human in every way and she had a smile on her face. Feeling a little nervous at seeing her there I very timidly walked down the three stairs and along the passage towards her. As I did so she began to walk forward as if to meet me, then gently went backwards, facing me all the time, until she reached the door of a small room at the end of the passage. On reaching it, to my surprise, she disappeared backwards through the closed door.'

Intrigued to know what on earth was happening, Gertrude Dancy forgot her nervousness and immediately went to the door, opened it and entered the room; but there was no trace of the figure she had seen seconds earlier, disappear into the room. The room was completely devoid of anyone, other than herself, and Mrs Dancy told me that she never forgot the experience and, more than thirty years later, she was completely confident and absolutely satisfied that she had indeed seen an unexplained figure.

When I talked to Mr Falloon about Mrs Dancy's experience he told me that in 1920 four friends visited Southfleet Rectory from Bath and while they were standing together, waiting for a key to be fetched to unlock a door on the landing where Gertrude had seen the ghost, they all saw a female figure come out of the Monks Room. The figure appeared to be perfectly normal and they did not take particular notice of it as it walked some forty-two feet along the passage, turned the corner at which they were standing, and, going to a door at the end of the landing, opened the door, passed inside, and closed the door behind it. Imagine their surprise and consternation when the key arrived, for which they had been waiting, to find that it was the key to the door through which the figure had apparently opened and closed, after passing through; a door which they all agreed once the key was to hand, was in fact securely locked!

The Rev. G.A. Bingley, former Rector of Burstow, was curate at Southfleet from 1923 until 1926, and during that period he resided at the rectory. One evening Mr Bingley and his wife (then his fiancée) saw a 'shadowy shape' at the end of a passage about thirty feet away from where they stood on the landing above the main staircase. The form appeared in a passage leading from the Monks Room. On almost every occasion that this apparition has been seen, it has apparently come out of the Monks Room. A solitary exception was mentioned to me by Mr Falloon concerning the wife of a former rector who once reported seeing the figure in the act of *entering* the Monks Room.

Mr Bingley told me of two further apparently paranormal happenings. An aunt of a former rector's wife saw a similar figure to that glimpsed by Mr Bingley and his wife, taking shape in the dining-room in daylight; and a nursemaid once reported seeing a figure on the landing above the main staircase one evening that could not be accounted for. She described the form she saw as a 'nurse with flowing veil' and said 'she' crossed the landing with a 'smiling look' and disappeared through a closed door.

At noon on 7th February 1942 the Rev. W.M. Falloon was standing in the hall at Southfleet Rectory when he suddenly became aware that a figure of a nun was standing between him and the window. He described her to me as being about four feet seven inches in height; dumpy in shape and dressed in a brown serge overall dress; similar to contemporary nuns' black apparel; with a brown tippet reaching to the elbows, and wearing a close-fitting brown serge cap.

Southfleet Rectory occupies the site of a former friary and tradition asserts that a nun found in the company of a monk inside the friary was bricked-up alive in the cellars. Stories of the reputed bricking-up of nuns is not infrequently encountered in haunted houses where the ghost figure of a nun has been seen although there is very sparse evidence to suggest that such a barbarous punishment was ever actually meted out in this country. However, on more than one occasion bones, believed to be those of a female person, have been found in suspicious circumstances that lend substance to such stories, as for example in the former deanery at Exeter where human bones were found between two walls of a bricked-up archway. Some of the walls at Southfleet Rectory are five feet six inches thick, out of which cupboards and alcoves have been fashioned and it is not beyond the realms of possibility that there are undiscovered human remains walled-up somewhere within the property. There has long been a tradition that the house had a room with no door, but this probably stems from the small powder closet, off a bedroom, where years ago occupants had their wigs powdered.

When I talked with Mr Falloon about the possible bricking-up of nuns, he told me that about a hundred years ago the west door of Southfleet church was badly blocked with dirt and rubble and after the churchwardens had cleared it, they uncovered the stone lid of a sarcophagus in the pathway. This was removed to the Scadbury pew inside the church and Mr Falloon pointed out to me an inscription around the edge stating that it marked the burial place of an excommunicated monk. Perhaps, as so often happens, a grain of truth is to be found in legend, and a nun and monk are indeed the chief actors in this drama.

Some years after I first talked with Mr Falloon he informed me that no paranormal activity had taken place at Southfleet Rectory since the appearance that he witnessed in 1942. There is a theory that hauntings, like batteries, run down after a while, and perhaps the Southfleet apparition, after some seventy or eighty years, ran its course.

When I knew Southfleet Rectory it was a wonderful old house, one wing Georgian, the centre Elizabethan and the other wing fourteenth century. The dining-room, once the refectory, was so well preserved, I remember, with a small bedroom above, furnished and decorated in period style, that one could easily picture the monks at their trenchers amid a sense of peace that was not of this world . . . and then there was the mystery of the underground passage. There had long been a story that a passage led from the rectory to a house known as The Limes and in the larder at Southfleet Rectory, where there were original oak shelves three inches thick and some very old tiles, traces of a spiral staircase could well have led to a secret underground passage.

I understand that the property is now divided into two separate dwellings, known as the Old Friary and Friary Court; the Old Friary comprising what was once the haunted part of the building. I have heard nothing of any ghosts or ghostly activity there for many years now.

## Sundridge

There is a lonely old house here called Combe (or Coombe) Bank, a house that probably goes back to Roman days; it used to be open to the public before it became a convent school.

Here, where a group of cedars of Lebanon are said to be unsurpassed anywhere in the country, a tragic story is told that seems to have resulted in the three-hundred-and-fifty acre park being haunted.

The young Earl Ferrers of the day was married to a countess and she appeared to be distraught when the Earl was arrested for the murder of his steward, who had given evidence against him in a petition for divorce, brought by Lady Ferrers. He was to be hanged at Tyburn although he hoped it might be Tower Hill where his ancestor, Queen Elizabeth's Essex, had been executed. 'I think it hard,' he said, 'that I must die at the place appointed for the execution of common felons'. He put on a brave show, however, dressing himself in his wedding clothes and driving to the place of execution in a carriage drawn by six horses and accompanied by a company of grenadiers, a sheriff in another carriage 'plentifully decked with ribbons', a troop of horses and, bringing up the rear, a mourning coach-and-horses.

As he progressed he conversed with the enormous crowd that had gathered to watch the flamboyant affair. To draw such a crowd for such an occasion, he said, was ten times worse than death but he supposed they never saw a lord hanged before and were unlikely to see another. Before he died however, he cursed his wife and hoped she would suffer a death more painful than his own. She subsequently married Lord Frederick Campbell and eventually died a very painful death, being burned in a fire in the tower of Combe Bank, and so severe and complete was the fire that all of her that was ever found in the ruins after the consuming fire was extinguished, was the bone of one thumb, which is buried here.

Small wonder that the ghost of Lady Frederick Campbell walked for many years amid the scenes she shared with two husbands and where she was virtually consumed in flames of terrifying ferocity.

## Tonbridge

Among the ghosts here is that of an unidentified lady in a large hat who haunts the Cardinal's Error in Lodge Oak Road on the outskirts of the town; and a black-and-white Tudor house where the ghost of a noble old collie dog has been seen by successive inhabitants, most often in the summer twilight 'sitting sedately under a walnut tree' on the lawn — 'real' dogs are invariably aware and respectful of the ghost dog and his locale, usually making a detour, with their tails down, whenever they pass near 'his' tree.

The ghost of The Cardinal's Error, so-named from Cardinal Wolsey's mistaken faith in Henry VIII, haunted one particular bedroom and when the daughter of a licencee slept there as a little girl, she asked her mother about the lady who used to come and sit at the bottom of her bed, a woman who always wore a big hat. Later, when the room was occupied by a guest, he said he would never be able to sleep in that room again because he was disturbed by the ghostly form of a woman who came into the room and sat at the bottom of his bed; a sad-looking, middle-aged woman who wore a large hat.

On many occasions, when the ghost has not been seen, the sound has been heard of someone walking along the corridor towards that particular bedroom; and other 'weird' sounds have been reported in various parts of the inn and, very occasionally, movement of objects. Once some toby jugs hanging over the bar began to swing by themselves, almost as though someone was touching them.

Kevin Griffin tells me that he unearthed one or two interesting items during the course of investigations into ghostly matters in the area. In the fifteenth century, when the Cardinal's Error was a farmhouse, nearby there was a priory that Wolsey certainly knew and visited. There are stories that Wolsey eventually took refuge at this priory when he was on the run from Henry VIII and that he escaped from the priory to the farmhouse, later the inn.

Kevin Griffin poses the question: could the lady who haunts the inn be a nun dressed in the cardinal's clothes, which might have helped him to escape and could have resulted in her death at the inn, perhaps by mistake, for anyone seeing the cardinal's robes would naturally think it *was* the cardinal. It is interesting that careful examination of the inn sign shows the cardinal wearing the usual red robes and soup-plate hat which, worn by a lady, could be described as 'wide-brimmed'; and the features of the cardinal appear to be more than a little effeminate!

Kevin Griffin has also reminded me that in the days when hop fields used to lie off the London road near Tonbridge in the 1920s, people working in the fields reported seeing on several occasions what was described as a 'white apparition'. The police were called in when the hop pickers became too frightened to go to work. The mystery seemed to be solved when a group of Tonbridge school boys admitted playing practical jokes and yet over the years there have been similar, admittedly infrequent, sightings of a similar nature in the same area.

In 1975 a gatehouse in the vicinity that was once owned by the railway was the scene of repeated sightings of a mysterious phantom girl. Officials from the railway visited the area in an effort to solve the mystery but they were unsuccessful.

The occupants at that time claimed to see the head and shoulders of a teen-age girl with fair hair inside the old building and several visitors, who knew nothing of the reputed ghost, said they felt uncomfortable in the gatehouse and thought there was 'something strange' about it. Sometimes the occupants of one particular room would experience the overwhelming impression that someone else was in the room, someone invisible but unmistakably there and watching. Soon doors and windows began to open and close by themselves and even the television set seemed to be affected by 'powerful static'. Then, as so often happens, the disturbances became less frequent, almost as though the power had run down, and soon there was peace and quiet in the lonely little gatehouse that might have some stories to tell if only it could talk.

## Tunbridge Wells

The High Street has several allegedly haunted properties including a shop where phantom footsteps walk up stairs that no longer exist; a house where an unidentified lady in a poke bonnet has been seen by successive occupants over a period of seventy years; and a corner property where a ghostly form has been seen looking out of an upstairs window — and the same form has been seen from the property opposite.

Also, if we are to believe the convincing evidence of a local resident, on at least one occasion some of the property in the region of the High Street has reverted to what it had been many years earlier!

One sunny June morning in 1968 Mrs Charlotte was doing some shopping in a store she did not normally use when she came across an archway which she discovered led to a small restaurant. She found herself in a dark room containing a number of tables with two women in rather long dresses and perhaps half-a-dozen men, all in dark suits, sitting at various tables, drinking coffee and chatting, although on reflection Mrs Charlotte could not remember hearing any sound. She was mildly surprised that she did not know the place existed but she had arranged to meet her husband so she did not stop but told herself she would bring her husband there at the next opportunity.

That opportunity presented itself the following week and Mrs Charlotte was very puzzled when she was unable to locate the restaurant or even the archway leading to it and when her husband made enquiries they were told that the shop had never been a restaurant. Mrs Charlotte was certain she was in the right shop and after a fruitless search for any room resembling the restaurant she had seen, she eventually discovered that a cinema had once stood on the site and in those days there had been a restaurant attached.

Mr and Mrs Charlotte were by this time intrigued as to what could have happened and they succeeded in tracing a man who had once owned the property adjoining the cinema and he confirmed that a coffee room had been approached through a doorway much as Mrs Charlotte described. The room had been rather dark and it had consisted of a bar with tables, exactly the room in which Mrs Charlotte had found herself a week earlier!

Ghost Clubber Dr A.R.G. Owen looked into the story and said at the time 'retrospective clairvoyance is a good deal rarer than ordinary contemporaneous clairvoyance and there is no real explanation for it'.

To the west of the town the area of Rusthall and Hurst Wood is known to have been occupied by Cromwellian forces during the Civil War and they may have left a ghostly headless horseman which has often been reported as seen on a pathway leading from Broomhill Road.

In 1966 a resident was walking here one evening when he became aware of the sound of approaching horses' hooves coming up behind him. He turned round and was astonished to see a horse carrying a headless rider bearing down on him. He just managed to jump to one side and to notice that the rider was wearing some sort of armour before the figure quickly passed him and disappeared.

Broomhill Road itself has a ghost. It is that of a man who appears to be standing in a hollow at the side of the road. The form was clearly seen by Mr and Mrs Philip Gearing of Tonbridge some years ago as they were motoring along the road. So near did the figure seem that both of them thought they must have struck the figure and they immediately stopped the car and searched but they could find nothing to account for what they had seen.

Enquiries elicited the fact that elderly residents could recall a large house and a cottage once standing at the exact spot where the figure had been seen; properties that were long regarded as haunted and in fact both the house and the cottage had stood empty for many years about the turn of the century because of the ghost of a man who haunted the area. One resident recalled that his family had known the people who had lived in the cottage and the occupants stated that they 'frequently' saw the figure and said the cottage was undoubtedly haunted.

An interesting ghost sighting was reported by Kim Waller, a reporter on a local paper, in 1969. He said he and a friend were sheltering from the rain late one evening beneath some trees on the Common when they suddenly became aware that what appeared to be two people, walking close together, were approaching from about fifty yards away. As the form came nearer they saw that the massive shape was one individual, 'tremendously broad around the middle and clothed in a long grey gown with what looked like frills around the bottom'.

The startled couple were unable to distinguish any limbs whatever and there was nothing but a dark shadow where the head should have been. As the strange form grew nearer still, it suddenly seemed to stumble and squatted in a crouching position only a few yards from the watchers. It remained there for several seconds, swaying and bobbing about and making a squelching noise, as might be made by someone wearing rubber boots that were filled with water. As the couple prepared to approach the figure, it moved slowly away and although the couple followed, it soon vanished and they could find no trace of anything to account for what they had seen.

The curator of the local museum was intrigued by the story and suggested that the figure may have been the ghost of a local character, enormous Mary Jennings, a drunkard who died when she was about thirty in 1736. She was described by a contemporary as 'not unlike a barrel'.

Other apparent hauntings in the locality include phantom footsteps in a period house in Calverley Park which have been heard by the occupants, walking about in a room on the floor above, when there has been nobody else in the house; and a phantom coach-and-horses that is supposed to career down Auckland Road, thought to date from an accident more than a century ago when the driver of such a vehicle, leaving a party at Charity Farm, lost control of the horses and the terrified beasts crashed the coach and killed all the occupants.

In Woodbury Park Road there used to be a home for orphaned children, some of whom were burnt to death in a fire. For some years afterwards local people and visitors reported hearing the sound of a childrens' choir coming from the gutted building. Twenty years after the fire, when the property was a private residence, the sound of singing continued to be reported from time to time together with irregular thumps and bangs and at one time an investigation into the disturbances was conducted but still the sounds were heard on occasions.

## West Peckham

It is some years since I was here in this perfectly delightful corner of the county with its village green, restful trees, and colourful barns and oasthouses, but at that time on a hill above the village stood the burned-out ruins of a cottage.

Here, if we are to believe stories handed down for generations, lived Jack Diamond, a highwayman; and here, one Friday the 13th, he burned to death in the cottage that always bore his name, Diamond's Cottage.

His ghost has been reputedly seen here on numerous occasions but only on that supposedly unluckiest of days, Friday the 13th. According to Antony Coxe ghosts walked here on 13th May 1961 at 6.30 a.m., a Friday, and a correspondent informs me that the ghost of Jack Diamond appeared here again as recently as 13th May 1983.

## Westerham

Many are the charms of Westerham; natural ones such as the hill on which it stands and the delightful scenes and walks across the Weald; and man-made ones: the timbered cottage where Pitt lived, beautifully proportioned Squerryes Court containing many interesting mementoes of General James Wolfe, 'Wolfe of Canada' who knew every yard hereabouts as a boy including Quebec House, where he lived; and Chartwell, beloved home of Sir Winston Churchill who bought the place in 1922 and which, except for the war years, was his home for the rest of his life.

I know of no ghost at Pitts Cottage or at Squerryes Court for that matter. The owner of the latter house is the present Lord of the Manor of Westerham and for more than two centuries now the Warde family have lived at the house, that is a typical example of a William and Mary manor house although in fact it was built in the reign of Charles II. I asked the present owner, Mr John St A. Warde whether there were any legends or ghost stories concerned with the house and in his reply (22nd July 1983) he says: ' . . . I have given the matter some thought, but have not come up with anything to connect Squerrys with a ghost story or other legend. The present house was built three hundred years ago and is light and airy in character. There was a previous mediaeval manor house on the site, but unfortunately we have no record of that house'.

There is, at Squerrys, in the dining-room, a fascinating seventeenth century Indo-Portuguese chest made in Goa about the time the house was built. Ebonised, pictured inside and out with religious subjects and inlaid with mother of pearl, it is thought to depict the story of Our Lady of Guadalupe. I quote from the Squerrys Court guidebook: 'Our Lady appeared to Juan Diego in 1531 on Tepeyac Hill where her shrine now stands. Juan Diego saw Our Lady several times and each time she asked him to report to the Bishop what he had seen. But the Bishop was sceptical and told Juan to ask Our Lady for a sign. Our Lady then told the young Italian to go to a certain place normally arid and barren, and gather roses from the hillside. He found a profusion of roses on the hill and brought them back. Our Lady arranged them in his mantle and told him to deliver them, undisturbed, to the Bishop. When the mantle was opened it had painted on it a life sized figure of Our Lady'.

Chartwell, furnished much as it was during Churchill's lifetime, seems to quietly exude the dynamic aura of the great man and it is hardly surprising that the unmistakable ghostly form of Sir Winston has been seen here, as Robin Fedden recounts in his *Churchill and Chartwell* (1968). My own enquiries support the generally accepted idea that the studio in the garden, where he was perhaps more relaxed than anywhere else, where some of his paintings adorn the walls, and where he spent so many happy hours, is probably more haunted than any other part of the place.

Randolph, Sir Winston's only son, has described one occasion when he distinctly saw his dead father in the room where a white marble bust of Lady Churchill stands near an old leather armchair. Randolph saw his father sitting in this armchair and, he always claimed, had a long discussion with him concerning men and events and the dangers that had overtaken the world since Sir Winston had died in 1965.

Many visitors to Chartwell are conscious of the somewhat disconcerting atmosphere of the very dominant personality who lived there and who has left behind a beautiful house and an intangible remnant of himself.


## Willesborough

The manor house of Boys Hall, built some three hundred years ago, has a remarkable front, looking rather like an abbey. The property has been much altered over the years but a convent or religious establishment of some kind may have occupied the site at one time.

The ghosts here, if ghosts there be, would appear to originate in an odd story long associated with the house. It is said that more than two centuries ago the son of the house was betrothed to one Ellen Scott who, at a party at the house, met and fell in love with a handsome individual named Tracey, much to the annoyance and indeed blind anger of her fiance who insisted on the agreed marriage taking place. Meanwhile the mysterious Tracey completely disappeared and during the years that followed Ellen and her husband spent a lot of time abroad where she eventually became a widow.

One night the then occupants of Boys Hall were startled to hear a loud knocking on the front door of the house, accompanied by pitiful moaning noises and heart-rending sobs. On opening the door they were astonished to find Ellen, distraught, clad only in a thin white dress and mumbling about still looking for her true love, Tracey . . .

She stumbled into the house, staggered up the stairs and disappeared into a bedroom. The occupants looked at one another: surely the poor girl had lost her reason — suddenly screams echoed through the great house and they rushed upstairs to find Ellen ranting and raving beside a secret hiding place she had exposed by removing some floor boards. Inside were the remains of a human being dressed as Tracey had once been dressed . . . and a bullet dropped from the skull when it was moved.

Before anyone could stop her Ellen had rushed to a window and jumped to her death. At a subsequent inquest on the two bodies the startling announcement was made that the remains of Tracey were those of a female! Small wonder that odd happenings have been reported from time to time at Boys Hall. A figure in white gliding noiselessly in one of the bedrooms; footsteps sounding along a corridor and down a stairway; inexplicable sounds emanating from empty rooms; a padding sound; a crashing and hammering noise; sounds of sighing and heavy breathing; and occasional 'touchings' in one of the upper rooms. The haunting of Boys Hall is as much a mystery as the history of the place itself and those who once lived there.

## Wittersham

This sleepy village where the iguanodon roamed ten million years ago, for bones of this prehistoric creature have been found here, does not worry overmuch about its ghost.

Over the last twenty years there have been at least a dozen reports of the figure of a little old woman, wearing a dark cloak, walking across the road towards Poplar Farmhouse, but she vanishes before she reaches the gate. Andrew Green says she appears to come from the entrance of Sweatman's Cottage and he wonders whether she can have any connection with the murder of a man in a nearby house about a century and a half ago.

One reliable witness is reported to have seen the figure twice within a few years and all those who have seen the mysterious lady say the figure appears to be quite solid and lifelike and there is nothing very remarkable or unusual about her, until she suddenly and inexplicably disappears.

## Wrotham

There is a century-old ghost story here that was sent to Lord Halifax and which he reproduced in his famous *Ghost Book*. It came from Mrs Brooke, wife of Major Alured de Vere Brooke, Royal Engineers, and corroborative evidence was obtained from a nurse.

In the autumn of 1879 the Brookes were invited to spend a couple of nights with some friends at Wrotham House, an old place of historic interest. The weather was cold and they drove over in their carriage, arriving just in time to dress for dinner and accordingly they were shown straight to their rooms. These were situated at the end of a long passage, up a short flight of stairs, and in a distant wing of the old house. The large bedroom was unconnected with the dressing-room which was a few paces down the passage. Although a fire was burning the bedroom seemed excessively cold and Mrs Brooke asked for extra wraps which were provided.

After dinner there was entertainment and dancing with the result that it was nearly two o'clock before the Brookes eventually retired for the night. Neither that night, nor the following one, when they were again late in retiring, did they get any rest. In spite of a fire and considerable clothing they were both 'horribly cold' and Brookes told his wife that he would not sleep another night in the room. They decided between them that the intense coldness must be due to damp mattresses and the fact that the room had probably not been used for some time; the thought of a possibly supernatural cause did not occur to them.

The following spring the Brookes were again invited to Wrotham, this time for a week, together with their little daughter aged five. Although her husband was unable to accompany them, due to his service duties, Mrs Brooke went with the little girl, who had been ill, as it was thought the change might do her good. She also took with her a nurse for the child.

Remembering the previous visit Mrs Brooke wrote beforehand and asked that the rooms might be thoroughly warm and the mattresses aired. Arriving on a Saturday and intending to stay until the following Saturday, Mrs Brooke found that the same rooms had been allocated as before and she arranged for her daughter to sleep with her and for the nurse to occupy the dressing-room.

That first night Mrs Brooke sat up late chatting to her hostess and she later recalled that as she passed through the hall on the way to her bedroom, somewhere a clock chimed one o'clock. As soon as she entered her bedroom she was struck by the intense coldness but she was relieved to find that her little girl did not appear to be affected by the coldness and was sleeping soundly. Nevertheless for more than an hour after she had lain down beside her daughter, Mrs Brooke shivered and shook with the cold.

At eight o'clock on the Sunday morning the nurse came in with a white face, red eyes and looking very frightened. She explained that she had had a very bad night and that up to about one o'clock someone had been playing practical jokes in the passage, 'opening her door, laughing outside, and then going away and coming back . . . ' Twice the nurse had locked her door but on each occasion she had shortly afterwards found it open again. Mrs Brooke decided the girl must have been dreaming and told her she should be more careful about what she ate before retiring for the night.

After breakfast the nurse took Mrs Brooke on one side and said: 'Oh, ma'am, is it not too bad? These rooms are haunted and the doors can never be kept shut before one o'clock!' It transpired that the servants had questioned her as to what sort of a night she had spent and when she told them they had said she need not be afraid another night as she had only to leave her door open and nothing would happen.

On the way back from church later that morning Mrs Brooke questioned her hostess about the house, asking which was the oldest part and so on, and whether there was a haunted room. Immediately she was aware of having touched on a sensitive subject and yes, she was told, there is a haunted room 'but we will not tell you which it is, as you might imagine things.' 'I think I know already,' replied Mrs Brooke. 'My nurse was frightened last night'.

She was unable to gain any further information however, but it was arranged that an under-housemaid would sleep with the nurse, if she was feeling worried. This was agreed and on retiring that night Mrs Brooke told the girls to leave the door of the room open and to go to sleep without thinking about ghosts — for she was sure there were no such things.

Mrs Brooke then went to her own room, undressed and sat in front of the fire, warming herself before getting into bed. She stresses that she was not feeling in the least nervous or apprehensive, but was rather curious as to what might happen that night. Feeling warmed, she decided against sitting up and having made up the fire, she locked the door and took the further precaution of putting a chair under the handle; then she went to bed and was soon asleep.

She found herself awake after what seemed a short time and she heard a clock strike midnight. Although she tried to go to sleep again she found herself getting colder and colder and soon sleep was impossible. She lay in bed waiting for whatever might happen.

Soon she heard footsteps coming along the passage and up the stairs and as they slowly approached her bedroom door she felt more and more alarmed. She told herself to be sensible and even prayed fervently.

She then heard a slight fumbling, as it were, with the handle of the door, which then opened quite noiselessly. A pale light, distinct from the firelight, streamed in, and then she saw the figure of a man who appeared to be clothed in a grey suit trimmed with silver and wearing a cocked hat. He walked into the room and stood by the side of the bed furthest from Mrs Brooke, with his back to her and facing the window. Mrs Brooke lay, scarcely daring to breathe, and in utter terror watched as he turned and still with his back to her, went out of the room uttering, as he did so, a horrid little laugh which seemed to freeze her blood. She heard his footsteps walk some paces down the passage and then heard him returning . . . At this point Mrs Brooke thinks she must have fainted for it was nearly two o'clock before she became fully conscious again. She did not get up immediately but lay there, thinking she must have had a dreadful dream, and trying to go back to sleep.

When daylight came the maid opened the bedroom door and pushed aside the chair that was still wedged against it.

The following evening Mrs Brooke asked her nurse, who had spent an undisturbed night, to come and sleep on the sofa in her bedroom. She did not tell the girl what she had seen or thought she had seen and she still found she had the courage to be interested enough to discover whether the events of the previous night would be repeated. That night, when she again heard a clock strike midnight, she called in a whisper to the nurse and found that she was also awake and presently they both began to feel very cold. Presently the nurse whispered that she could hear footsteps and Mrs Brooke, who also heard them, said she would get up and see who it was.

She tried to get up, and then tried again, but it was no use. It was as though she was bound to the bed — and she felt all her courage leaving her. Once again the door opened noiselessly and the grey figure made his entry and uttered his diabolical little laugh. The nurse saw and heard all this exactly as did Mrs Brooke and she too said she found herself unable to move from the sofa while the happenings were taking place.

Next day Mrs Brooke told the lady of the house what had happened and said that since she did not feel she could spend such another night, she had decided to go home. In vain she was told that she would not be disturbed again; that the ghost only appeared three times and always to strangers and never did any harm. But Mrs Brooke had had enough and she left the house and as she put it, 'forfeited a friendship' in doing so.

She told Lord Halifax that she understood the family had suffered such visitations for seventy-five years and that the ghost was supposed to be that of a man who murdered his brother in the room in which she had slept and had then thrown his body out of the window. She was told that there was in existence a portrait of one of the brothers, dressed as she described him. Mrs Brooke included with her story a note from the nurse, Miss C.E. Page, confirming the experience and this Lord Halifax reproduced in his book.